NEW FROM TOM RATH IN 2015

FULLY CHARGED: *THE MOVIE*

Fully Charged features the world's leading experts on behavioral health (Brian Wansink), the psychology of spending (Ryan Howell), social networks (Nicholas Christakis), decision making and behavioral economics (Thomas Gilovich), willpower (Roy Baumeister), and the role of meaning in our work (Amy Wrzesniewski). The film also follows individuals and organizations who are transforming themselves and their communities. You will hear from a company where employees work on treadmill desks; a church that gave its members $500 to spend on others; a "guerilla gardener" who plants vegetables in South Central LA's abandoned lots; the US Army Surgeon General; and the co-founder of an organization that has helped thousands of low-income students make it to college. Filled with expertise and provocative real-world stories, *Fully Charged* reveals some of the most practical ways we can all energize our work and life.

THE RECHARGEABLES

From Tom Rath, the co-author of *How Full is Your Bucket? For Kids*, the book that started a conversation about the importance of positive interactions in schools and homes around the world, comes a timeless story about how to be healthy and create energy in our daily lives. Through a series of brief adventures, Poppy and Simon discover what it takes to recharge themselves and bring an entire village back to life.

EAT MOVE SLEEP: *2015 EDITION WITH NEW WELBE APP*

An updated 2015 edition of the *New York Times* bestseller that includes access to Welbe, a new mobile app for tracking how you eat, move, and sleep in one central place. Welbe allows you to connect with friends across platforms (e.g., Android, iOS) and wearable devices (e.g., Fitbit, Jawbone, Garmin).

PRAISE FOR
ARE YOU FULLY CHARGED?

"Tom Rath's books — which include *StrengthsFinder 2.0* and *Eat Move Sleep* — have sold 6 million copies and spent 300 weeks on the *Wall Street Journal* bestseller list. This one is arguably Rath's best. He has written a book that is as readable as it is rigorous and as profound as it is practical."

—DANIEL H. PINK, author of
Drive and *To Sell Is Human*

"*Are You Fully Charged?* is about renewing ourselves in the fullest sense. Drawing on his extensive research, Tom Rath provides us with the three key pillars that can help create a life of more meaning and perspective: being part of something larger than ourselves, valuing people and experiences over mere stuff, and understanding that looking after our own well-being is the first step to doing more for others. An essential book for anyone wanting more out of life."

—ARIANNA HUFFINGTON, author of
Thrive and co-founder of *The Huffington Post*

"Tom Rath's brilliant new book, *Are You Fully Charged?*, builds on his mega best-selling StrengthsFinder series to show you can lead a more meaningful life that results in more energy and better interactions every day. If you follow Rath's wise counsel and adopt his practical advice, your life will be more fulfilling and rewarding."

—BILL GEORGE, author of
True North and former CEO of Medtronic

"How to live? That is the question — and Tom Rath has the answer. In his important new book, *Are You Fully Charged?*, Rath draws on his decades of research — and his deep humanity — to point you in the right direction, and to instill your journey with joy and meaning."

—SUSAN CAIN, author of
*Quiet: The Power of Introverts in a
World That Can't Stop Talking*

"*Are You Fully Charged?* lays out a blueprint for a better life that creates more energy. Rath's book is easy to read, research-backed, and immediately practical."

—CHIP AND DAN HEATH,
authors of *Decisive, Switch*, and *Made to Stick*

"Once again, the brilliant Tom Rath has written an absolutely indispensable book. Here, he reveals how meaning, interactions, and energy are the three crucial elements that allow us to live happier, healthier, more productive lives. *Are You Fully Charged?* will inspire people to make changes, starting tomorrow morning."

—GRETCHEN RUBIN, author of
The Happiness Project and *Better Than Before*

"Tom Rath reveals that engagement depends not on happiness but on meaning, interactions, and energy. This important, lucid book is full of fresh evidence that you can put into action to shift your motivation into a higher gear."

—ADAM GRANT, Wharton professor
and author of *Give and Take*

ARE YOU FULLY CHARGED?

THE 3 KEYS
TO ENERGIZING YOUR
WORK AND LIFE

TOM RATH

silicon_guild

Library of Congress Control Number: 2014960258
ISBN: 978-1-939714-03-9 (hardcover edition)
ISBN: 978-1-939714-05-3 (digital edition)
ISBN: 978-1-939714-06-0 (international paperback edition)
ISBN: 978-1-939714-07-7 (international digital edition)

First Printing: 2015
10 9 8 7 6 5 4 3 2 1

Bulk purchase discounts, special editions, and customized excerpts are available direct from the publisher. For information about books for educational, business, promotional purposes, or any other requests, please email: **inquiries@missionday.com**

To book this author for a speaking engagement, contact the Missionday Speakers Bureau: **speaking@missionday.com**

Author's website: **www.tomrath.org**

To my mother, Connie Rath,
who has spent a lifetime creating a positive charge
for others

CONTENTS

CONTENTS

PART III: ENERGY

CREATING A POSITIVE CHARGE: TOOLS AND RESOURCES   163

ARE YOU
FULLY CHARGED?

Prologue:
Are You Fully Charged?

When you are fully charged, you get more done. You have better interactions. Your mind is sharp, and your body is strong. On days when you are fully charged, you experience high levels of engagement and well-being. This charge carries forward, creating an upward cycle for those you care about.

I am far more effective in my work on days when I am fully charged. I am also a better husband, dad, and friend. Most notably, I can do more for others. However, until recently, it was unclear to me what specific actions create this daily charge.

I've spent my entire career studying workplace engagement, health, and well-being. While I have written several books on these topics, the greatest challenge I have faced personally is how to integrate findings from my research into my own daily routine. After all, knowledge does little good unless I can change my behaviors.

Fortunately, a new body of research has recently emerged that focuses on the topic of creating *daily* well-being. Historically, asking people questions and tracking their actions was time-consuming and expensive. As a result, researchers gathered broad, general information about people's lives and work. Most research on well-being over the past century was based on asking people about their lives over the span of years or decades.

When people are asked to reflect on an entire lifetime, the first things they think of are broad concepts like health and wealth. The problem is, these general measures are not very practical for improving people's lives on a daily basis. Health is the sum of many years. Wealth is not created in a span of days. This is why a different way of measuring what's important in life is crucial.

The Science of Daily Experience

The time and cost of tracking what people do are now remarkably low. It is much easier to measure thoughts, feelings, and behaviors on a daily, even momentary, basis. New technology enables scientists to ask people what they are doing at various times of the day, who they are with, and how much they enjoy an activity. Sensors and wearable devices can even measure how people are doing, with no input required from those wearing the devices.

These technologies, paired with innovative research methods, have led to a rapid expansion in knowledge about the central elements of daily well-being. Researchers call this *daily experience*, which is the product of positive and negative experiences (or positive and negative affect) throughout the day. Daily experience is measured by asking people whether they have emotions like happiness, enjoyment, stress, and other feelings *within a given day*. This distinction between daily well-being and broad evaluation of life satisfaction is important because it leads to very different conclusions about the best investment of time and resources.

Traditional measures of life satisfaction, for example, might suggest putting a great deal of energy into increasing your income. Yet, although life satisfaction scores continue to increase (almost indefinitely) with income, making more money does not actually change *daily experience* once people reach an income threshold.

In the United States, for example, daily well-being does not show *any* statistically significant increases after someone reaches $75,000 of annual household income. While this figure has received a good deal of attention, people tend to miss the fact that almost all of the gains in daily well-being associated with increases in income occur below the $40,000 level. Essentially, a certain income level is necessary for food, shelter, and preventing daily worries, but once you have reached that basic level of financial security, making more money is unlikely to lead to better days.

The study of daily well-being is also upending the conventional wisdom that wealthier countries have happier citizens. In the past, when scientists looked at life satisfaction, the wealthiest countries were consistently at the top of the national well-being rankings. But when Gallup asked people in 138 countries about their daily experience, the results told a very different story. The country with the highest "positive experience" score was Paraguay, a nation that ranks 105th in terms of its wealth (measured by GDP per capita). Among the top five countries on this daily well-being index, *four were in the bottom half* of the wealthiest countries list.

This research is encouraging to me because it suggests that daily well-being does not depend on accumulating riches or living in a wealthy country. The more I've learned about the difference between long-term evaluation and daily experience, the more I've grown to understand the importance of the latter. Personally, I care a lot more about laughing, smiling, and enjoying moments with my wife and kids today than how I might rate my overall life satisfaction 10 years from now. And trying to help people improve their day-to-day experiences is more practical than trying to improve their life satisfaction over time.

Your overall satisfaction with life certainly matters. But you create meaningful change in moments and days, not years and decades. It is easier to improve your own happiness — and the well-being of others — when you focus on doing it right now. Taking small, meaningful actions today is the best way to make changes. And eventually, these small changes will lead to important long-term outcomes.

The Three Keys to a Full Charge

To discover what creates a full charge, my team and I reviewed countless articles and academic studies, and interviewed some of the world's leading social scientists.* We identified and catalogued more than 2,600 ideas for improving daily experience. As we narrowed down the concepts to the most proven and practical strategies, underlying patterns continued to surface. Three key conditions differentiate days when you have a full charge from typical days:

- **Meaning**: doing something that benefits another person
- **Interactions**: creating far more positive than negative moments
- **Energy**: making choices that improve your mental and physical health

When we surveyed more than 10,000 people to see how they were doing across these three areas, we found that most people struggle on a daily basis. For example, when we asked them to think about their entire day yesterday, a mere *11 percent reported having a great deal of energy*. Clearly, most people are operating well below their capacity.

---

* To watch extended interviews with leading scientists featured in this book, or for direct links to all references from the appendix, visit tomrath.org

As a result, they are less effective in their work. Their interactions with friends and family are nowhere near as good as they could be. And their physical health worsens as days with too much stress and too little activity accumulate. It is time for this to change.

The good news is that you don't have to go on a retreat in the woods to find meaning, you don't need to find new friends at a cocktail party to have better interactions, and you certainly don't need to run a marathon or embark on a fad diet to create physical energy. The biggest changes for your daily well-being start with a few small steps.

20%
of people spent a lot of time doing
meaningful work yesterday

1

Create Meaning with Small Wins

What will you do *today* that makes a difference?

I started asking myself this question, rather intensively, when I was a teenager. Not because I was ahead of my time or enlightened, but as a result of my cancer diagnosis at age 16. After I lost sight in my left eye to a large tumor, my doctors suspected I had a rare genetic condition that shuts off a powerful tumor suppressor. The results of a blood test confirmed I had this VHL gene mutation, which leads to cancerous growth throughout the body. I essentially lost the genetic lottery.

My doctors told me I would need to spend a week in the hospital for scans and testing every year for the rest of my life. This allows my physicians to keep track of cancers — currently growing in my eye, kidneys, pancreas, adrenal glands, and spine — and to operate or try chemotherapy as needed. But if everything goes well, as it has most of the time, I leave the hospital at the end of that week with a fresh 12-month lease on life.

Having this extension — with terms that are renewed annually — energizes me to try to make a difference every single day. Thinking back to when I first received my diagnosis, what's most fascinating to me is how there was almost no negative effect on my daily well-being. If anything, having this constant threat has caused me to focus even more of my time on the little things that matter most in a given day.

It has now been 23 years since my diagnosis. And while I continue to live on somewhat borrowed time, I have spent most of my life working on what will outlast it. From research and writing to building relationships and playing with my kids, I see all of this time I spend as an investment in the future that can grow when I'm gone. Trying to create a little meaning each day has also kept me from dwelling on a genetic condition beyond my control. In the process, I have learned far more about living than I have worried about dying. The reality is, nobody knows if their lease on life will last for days, years, or decades.

Through both research and personal experience, I have discovered that creating meaning is central not just to my existence but to that of every organization in society today. Businesses, schools, governments, families, and faith-based groups are being challenged more than ever to show how they make a meaningful contribution to society. The essential thing people want in a job today is work that will allow them to create meaning for others. My research suggests that the odds of being completely engaged in your job increase by more than 250 percent if you spend a lot of time doing meaningful work throughout the day.

To discover what leads to better work and lives, Harvard Business School's Teresa Amabile and psychologist Steven Kramer sorted through 12,000 diary entries and 64,000 specific workday events collected from 238 workers across seven different companies. Their conclusion from this research was: "Of all the events that engage people at work, the single most important — by far — is simply making progress in meaningful work." This research also showed that creating meaning is an evolutionary process that grows by the day, as opposed to a grand purpose that suddenly falls in your lap.

Small wins generate meaningful progress. You might create a small positive charge for one of your customers today or work on a new product that will benefit people in the future. Over the weekend, maybe you'll have a long conversation with a loved one that makes a difference. It is these little moments, not grand actions, that create substance and meaning.

Abandon the Pursuit of Happiness

The pursuit of meaning — not happiness — is what makes life worthwhile. Despite Thomas Jefferson including it in the Declaration of Independence, the "pursuit of happiness" is a shortsighted aim. Putting *your own well-being* before *well-doing* pulls you in the wrong direction.

People who spend life seeking happiness are unlikely to find it. Much like chasing fame or wealth, seeking happiness alone is misguided and can lead to poor decisions.

Clearly, happiness is a positive condition. Being around people who have higher levels of well-being is more enjoyable than being around people who don't. It is the constant pursuit of *your own* happiness that leads you astray. Pursuing happiness for loved ones or for your community is a worthwhile goal. But trying to create happiness for yourself can have the opposite effect, according to recent studies.

Scientists are still uncovering the reasons why the pursuit of happiness backfires. Part of the explanation lies in its self-focused nature. Research suggests that the more value you place on your own happiness, the more likely you are to feel lonely on a daily basis. When participants in experiments were deliberately induced to value happiness more by reading a bogus article extolling the benefits of happiness, they reported feeling lonely. And samples of their saliva indicated corresponding decreases in progesterone levels — a hormonal response associated with loneliness. Seeking your own happiness and nothing else results in feelings of futility. But if you spend as much time creating meaningful interactions as you do pursuing happiness, you will be better off in both areas.

Swim in the Deep End of Life

Happiness and meaningfulness are two distinct human conditions. While there is some overlap, the differences have clear implications for how people spend their time. Those who pursue happiness, for example, are what psychologists calls "takers." As Roy Baumeister and his team noted after studying this topic extensively, "Happiness without meaning characterizes a relatively shallow, self-absorbed or even selfish life." In contrast, co-author Kathleen Vohs explained, "People leading meaningful lives get a lot of joy from giving to others."

Baumeister points out that it is not the pursuit of happiness but the pursuit of meaning that sets humans apart from animals. In some cases, creating meaning involves putting another person's needs before your own, which could lead to short-term decreases in your happiness. However, when you do, you make a contribution that improves the environment around you.

Happiness and meaningfulness also appear to have distinct influences on physiological health. When participants in a study led by the University of North Carolina's Barbara Fredrickson were happy but lacked meaning in their lives (defined as pursuing a purpose bigger than self), they exhibited a stress-related gene pattern that is known to activate an inflammatory response. They had the same gene expression pattern as people dealing with constant adversity have. Over time, this pattern leads to chronic inflammation, which is related to a host of illnesses, like heart disease and cancer. Fredrickson noted, "Empty positive emotions . . . are about as good for you as adversity."

Unfortunately, 75 percent of participants in Fredrickson's study fell into this category; their happiness levels outpaced their levels of meaningfulness. In contrast, participants who had meaning in their lives, whether or not they characterized themselves as happy, showed a *deactivation* in this stress-related gene pattern. In other words, their bodies did not act as if they were under constant duress and threat.

Participating in meaningful activities elevates your thinking above yourself and your own momentary needs. Every minute you can set aside your own happiness for the sake of others will eventually lead to stronger families, organizations, and communities. In the end, the pursuit of happiness and "success" will pass. What endures is creating meaning in your own life and in the lives of others.

2

Pursue Life, Liberty, and Meaningfulness

Historically, finding meaning has been portrayed as a personal journey — something you discover through extensive searching or call on in times of need. Finding a higher purpose in life is considered the ultimate existential and philosophical goal. The study of meaningfulness has been influenced by Viktor Frankl's landmark 1946 book *Man's Search for Meaning*, which chronicled his experience in a Nazi concentration camp. The book describes how finding something meaningful in the bleakest of human conditions allowed Frankl and others to survive. Surely a conclusion this substantial could come only from enduring such harrowing conditions, right?

As it turns out, Frankl's discoveries about meaning started years before he was forced into a concentration camp, when he was a medical student trying to prevent suicide in teenagers struggling with depression. Frankl developed a treatment that he called "logotherapy." The basic principle of this approach is to help people find practical goals and steps that create "specific and individual meaning." In Frankl's words, "Happiness cannot be pursued; it must ensue. One must have a reason to 'be happy.'" It was this work that he used as he helped fellow prisoners in concentration camps.

Frankl's initial theory about how young people find meaning is now being tested through carefully designed experiments. A 2014 study followed a group of teenagers for a full year to see how their brains reacted to self-fulfilling (hedonic) acts versus acts that created meaning (eudaimonic) using fMRI scans and questionnaires. While the participants were in the fMRI scanner, researchers posed scenarios to them about keeping money for themselves versus donating it to their families. The researchers also followed up at the end of the year to review any changes from the teens' baseline levels of depressive symptoms.

The results revealed that teenagers who had the greatest brain response to meaningful actions had the greatest declines in depressive symptoms over time. In contrast, teens who made more self-fulfilling decisions were more likely to have an increase in risk of depression. Meaningful activity essentially protects the brain from dark thoughts.

As Frankl observed in the early years of his career, people's need for meaningful work begins when they are young.

Get a Charge From Within

Meaningful work is driven by intrinsic, rather than extrinsic, motivation. *Extrinsic motivation* is a nice way of describing when you do things primarily to receive a reward. You might take a new job because of the higher pay and better benefits package. Then you work 60-hour weeks to reach an arbitrary goal that someone else has set. After all, it will look good on your résumé a few years from now when someone is judging you — based on their own motivations.

Intrinsic motivation — or deep internal motivation — is much richer. For example, consider a teacher who is inspired by the growth of a student or a doctor who is driven by improving health. Intrinsic motivation stems from the meaningfulness of the work you do. You are driven by what you yearn to do even if there is no reward or compensation.

Emerging research suggests that it is better to focus solely on intrinsic motivation, because *deriving any motive whatsoever from external incentives could decrease performance.* Yale's Amy Wrzesniewski and her team followed 11,320 West Point military cadets and assessed their motives for attending the academy over a 14-year period. The researchers made a startling discovery: Cadets who entered West Point because of internal motivators were more likely to graduate, become commissioned officers, receive promotions, and stay in the military compared with those who entered due to external motives. Those cadets who entered with both strong internal (e.g., a desire to lead others) and external (e.g., to get a better job and make more money) motives, however, did not exhibit that same likelihood of success.

Contrary to what these researchers initially suspected, *two* strong motivators led to *poorer* outcomes across all of these measures when compared with internal motivation alone. The results caused the researchers to question whether the Army should put more emphasis on leading others and serving your country instead of money for college or career training. They also questioned this general logic for other professions, like the practice of motivating teachers with bonuses for higher test scores.

"Helping people focus on the meaning and impact of their work, rather than on, say, the financial returns it will bring, may be the best way to improve not only the quality of their work but also — counterintuitive though it may seem — their financial success," observed Wrzesniewski and her co-author Barry Schwartz. This is especially important because it is easy to fall into the trap of allowing external incentives, such as monetary rewards at work, to detract from your ability to focus on meaningful efforts to serve others.

One challenge is that cultivating and developing intrinsic motivation often requires conscious effort. To study this, researchers randomly assigned groups of creative writers to take a survey that either subtly reminded them of intrinsic or extrinsic motivations for writing. If the writers thought about intrinsic reasons beforehand, their subsequent work was graded as far more creative. In contrast, when writers spent even five minutes thinking about the external motivators for their work, it had the opposite effect.

Think about the implications for your work. When you are bombarded with conventional carrot-and-stick motivators, even if they help at first, they are not sustainable. Instead, look for small ways to keep your best internal motivators top of mind throughout the day.

Just having photos of my kids on my smartphone lock screen and desk is a great reminder and motivator for me. A friend of mine in publishing is driven by a weekly report that shows how many people are reading the books he has worked on. James Allen, a train station attendant in London, motivates himself by trying to get even the most hardened commuters to smile. The things that charge you from within are likely very different from what works best for the people around you. Intrinsic motivations are not universal; they are individualized.

Try to find activities outside of work that appeal to your intrinsic motivation. One study found that employees who were encouraged to engage in creative activities *unrelated to work*, such as creative writing or other artistic endeavors, subsequently performed better *on the job*. Researchers at the University of Exeter found that simply being able to decorate your workspace with things like plants, art, or pictures of loved ones could increase productivity by up to 32 percent. This is why companies like Google encourage employees to make their workplace feel like home, even if it looks like a mess to others.

Forge Meaning in the Moment

Meaning does not happen to you — you create it. One of the most important elements of building a great career and life is attaching what you do each day to a broader mission. Until you understand how your efforts contribute to the world, you are simply going through the motions each day.

Creating meaning in your work does not require a grand plan about how you personally will alter the fate of the world. It can be much more practical — and relevant — to the people you care about most. Start by asking why your current job or role even exists. In most cases, jobs are created because they help another person, make a process more efficient, or produce something people need.

If you stock shelves at a grocery store, you are saving people time and making it easier for them to have nourishing meals at home with their family. Almost anyone who works in customer service or a call center has an opportunity to comfort someone, solve a problem, and improve another person's day. If you develop apps or software for a living, your products provide great utility, save time, entertain, or keep people connected. When you think about it, it's not that difficult to find meaningful aspects of almost any job.

Once you have identified how your efforts create a better life for others, consider what you could do to deliver a better product to the people you serve. Just think of all the different interactions you have had as a customer. When a customer service rep treats you and your request poorly, it can derail the rest of your day. On the other hand, if someone resolves your problem in a warm and understanding manner, the response gives you a positive charge and can turn a bad experience into a good one.

This is the type of daily impact you can have in your interactions with your friends, family, colleagues, and customers. But it takes effort to determine exactly how your interactions charge the environment around you every day. Start by attaching meaning to small interchanges. Over time, you will be able to connect the dots between your efforts and a larger purpose.

Most people I talk to have the opportunity to engage in meaningful pursuits on their own time. However, when I ask people about the meaningfulness of their work each day, they struggle with the question. To me, this is deeply concerning, given the fact that most people spend the majority of their waking hours dedicated to being full-time workers, students, parents, or volunteers.

3

Make Work a Purpose,
Not Just a Place

When Amy Wrzesniewski studied workers on the cleaning staff in a hospital system, she was amazed by how differently people viewed the same job. Some workers saw their job as a paycheck — a way to put food on the table and cover expenses. Others, meanwhile, considered their work to be a true calling.

When Wrzesniewski and her colleagues dug deeper, they found that these differences were not the result of what shift someone worked, the unit they worked on, or how long they had been on the job. Instead, the difference lay in whether or not a worker had strayed from their formal job description and become involved in meaningful interactions and relationships with patients and visitors. Those who had done this found greater meaning in their work. As one of the workers explained to Wrzesniewski, "I do everything I can to promote the healing of patients. Part of that is about creating clean and sterile spaces in which they can recover, but it also extends to anything else I can possibly do to facilitate healing." When these workers identified with being a part of the overall care team, it completely transformed their work and identity.

The work you do each day is how you make a difference in the world. You probably spend the majority of your time doing something that is considered a job, occupation, or calling. It is essential to make this time count. If you can find the right work, you can create meaning every day, instead of trying to squeeze the most important things in around the edges.

Work should be more than a necessary means to an end. Yet one dictionary lists "work" as synonymous with "drudgery" and "servitude." When I ask people about their career expectations, one of the most frequent replies I hear is, "You don't live to work; you work to live." The assumption built into this belief is that people work primarily for a paycheck in a job devoid of meaning.

While defining work as little more than a monetary transaction may have rung true a century ago, it is at best an incomplete description of what employees are looking for today. This type of transactional relationship is also directly at odds with what organizations require from employees in a modern economy. The last thing businesses need is employees who show up to punch a time clock and who give only a fraction of their energy and effort to the organization's mission.

The fundamental relationship between an employee and an organization is finally starting to change. When I was young, most adults I observed in the workplace were working hard primarily for the paycheck, trying to move as quickly as possible to the next step on a ladder, or working to the point of exhaustion so they could retire early. These efforts were usually rooted in good intentions or a strong work ethic. However, this dynamic is neither sustainable for individuals nor optimal for productivity.

Work for *More Than* a Living

The concept of bringing people together in groups, tribes, or organizations is based on the fundamental premise that human beings can do more collectively than they can in isolation. Hundreds of years ago, people banded together for the sake of sharing food and shelter and keeping their family safe. The basic assumption was that the association gained by joining a group would benefit individuals and their loved ones. As a species, humans are better off together than they are apart. Simple enough.

This is why I was taken aback by research Gallup conducted on this topic. When workers across the United States were asked whether their lives were better off because of the organization they worked for, a mere *12 percent* claimed that their lives were significantly better. The vast majority of employees felt their company was a *detriment* to their overall health and well-being.

How did this relationship between individuals and organizations go so wrong? One catalyst for this change was the Industrial Revolution, when people almost literally became cogs in big machines and assembly lines. The premise was that an employee would work at a routine task for a fixed number of hours in exchange for a set amount of hourly pay. While this led to a great deal of automation, innovation, and productivity growth, it also resulted in unintended side effects that linger today.

These transactional relationships made it easy for companies to work someone to the point of burnout, knowing they could hire the next person in line. Everything from organizational hierarchies to compensation structures sent a simple message: You are replaceable. At almost every turn, classic economics ruled. No one was even asking whether people's lives were better because they were part of a particular organization.

When I entered the workforce in the 1990s, the general expectation was not much different. A company offered you a job performing a specific task. If you completed that task, you earned a wage. Some jobs also provided benefits like health insurance, retirement funds, or other incentives to retain employees. A few companies even asked employees if they were satisfied with their jobs. However, these satisfaction levels have gotten progressively worse over the past 25 years.

Go Beyond Engagement

Near the start of the 21st century, some companies began asking if their employees were emotionally engaged (not just satisfied) with the work they were doing each day. These inquiries created a major shift; managers and leaders were finally paying attention to whether people were not just showing up but also giving all of their "discretionary effort" to the organization.

Employers are now quite savvy about whether you are engaged or disengaged while you are on the job. They know what the organization is *getting out of you*. However, in most cases, you do not know how, or even if, *your life is improving* because you are part of that organization.

This relationship needs to change for the foundational compact between individuals and organizations to succeed. The reality is: *What's good for an employee is in the organization's best interest as well*. A Towers Watson analysis of 50 global companies found that organizations with low scores on traditional engagement measures averaged a 10 percent operating margin. This went up to 14 percent among companies with high employee engagement scores. In organizations with "sustainable engagement," meaning the organization also improved employees' personal well-being, the average operating margin was greater than 27 percent.

This analysis suggests that your personal well-being is just as important as how engaged you are in your job, even if you look at things only from an employer's financial perspective. If you show up for work fully charged, it increases your engagement and leads to better interactions with your colleagues and customers. This is good for your peers, the people you serve, and the long-term interests of the organization.

A healthy relationship between an employee and an organization starts with a shared mission, meaning, or purpose. A 2013 study of more than 12,000 workers worldwide found that employees who derive meaning and understand the importance of their work are more than *three times* as likely to stay with an organization. Author Tony Schwartz described how this one element has "the highest single impact of any variable" in a study that looked at many elements of a great workplace. Meaningful work was also associated with 1.7 times higher levels of overall job satisfaction.

The future of work lies in redefining it as doing something that makes a difference each day. *Work is a purpose, not a place.* Work is about productively applying your talent. Work is about making your life, and the lives of other people, stronger as a product of your efforts. But getting to this point starts by moving beyond the pull of a paycheck.

4

Find a Higher Calling Than Cash

Working primarily for money is little more than a modern-day form of bribery. If another person is paying you to do what he wants you to do when you would rather be doing something else, that is not an ideal situation. The path of least resistance is to treat monetary compensation as the central element of the relationship between a person and an organization. But that sets both parties up for inevitable failure.

Countless studies have shown that nonfinancial incentives — such as recognition, attention, respect, and responsibility — can be more effective than financial incentives. People who wrap their identity around their annual income rarely find satisfaction in their work. Someone else will always have a bigger house or a better car. It is a race you will never win. Money and power can be used for great purposes, but they can also be a trap.

For me, keeping monetary incentives in perspective is an ongoing challenge. Every month, I sort through a wide range of opportunities to spend time with different groups or work on specific projects. If I based my decisions strictly on the economic benefit, it would make for much easier choices. However, while money does matter to an extent, it should not be the primary determinant when allocating time and effort. Instead of starting with classic economics to prioritize my time, I now begin by asking *how my time can make a difference for others.*

I have found that leading with this fundamental question, before delving into the financial aspects, usually leads to better choices. When I reflect on what I'm most proud of throughout my career, the first thing that comes to mind is a project I worked on in 2001 called StrengthsQuest. My task was to work with a small team at Gallup to create a book and online program that helped freshmen build their college experience around their natural talents.

More than a decade later, 2 million students have completed this program and are better equipped to find careers that capitalize on their strengths. I give an effort like this even more weight — in my informal calculus of creating meaning — because it is reaching students at such a critical time in their lives. Even though I was working behind the scenes as an IT project manager and could barely see the direct influence on students from that distance, the meaning

I derived from being a part of that effort continues to influence my choices today.

Avoid Upward Comparison

It's easy to think that doubling your income will lead you to an entirely different level of happiness. One national sampling found that Americans thought their overall life satisfaction would double if they went from making $25,000 a year to making $55,000 a year. When researchers looked at the actual differences in life satisfaction that a sudden doubling of income produced, it did boost happiness — by 9 percent. Nine percent is better than 0 percent, but, as one of the study's authors put it, "It's still kind of a letdown when you were expecting a 100 percent return."

It's important to note that financial security is vital to your well-being. Constant worry about being able to afford basic necessities or to pay off debt can lead to stress, fear, and uncertainty. Yet if you are able to reach a level of basic financial security, making more money becomes less important for your daily well-being. At much higher income levels, increases in annual pay are unlikely to produce any real effect.

Even at the highest end of the continuum, there are many millionaires who don't feel "rich enough" relative to their peers. A study conducted in the United Kingdom found that satisfaction and income are almost entirely relative to one's comparison group. One of the researchers summarized, "Earning a million pounds a year appears to be not enough to make you happy if you know your friends all earn 2 million a year." The challenge is to figure out how to avoid this game of upward comparison.

Judging the success of your career based on the amount of money you make can quickly lead you astray. Think of all the people you know who worked tireless hours at jobs that were less than enjoyable for decades. Behind the scenes, many of these seemingly "successful" people led pretty miserable lives because they failed to put things in perspective and work for meaning instead of a paycheck. Nobel Prize–winning psychologist Daniel Kahneman and his co-authors found that wealth can lead people to spend less time doing things that are enjoyable and more time doing things that create stress.

Unless dying with more money than anyone else in the cemetery is your ultimate goal, you need to evaluate the health of your career more broadly. Ask yourself a few basic questions: Are your relationships stronger because of your job? Is your physical health better because of the organization you are part of? Are you contributing more to society because of what you do every day?

Keep Money From Killing Meaning

Simply *thinking* about money can cause you to put your own interests ahead of the collective good. Even if you have the best intentions, once you are paid to outperform your peers (who are presumably given the same motivation), individual incentives create a division between you and your colleagues. Left unchecked, financial motivation can erode your well-being and relationships, and it can diminish your contribution to society.

A University of Minnesota study found that when participants were reminded of monetary rewards, they were *three times* more likely to prefer working alone to working with others. The same study revealed that in a social setting, the mere thought of money made people position their chairs roughly 12 additional inches apart. Participants literally moved away from other people and isolated themselves when money was on their minds. This is one reason why group incentives tend to work better, as they create more cohesion and less division.

The more you focus your efforts on others, the easier it is to do great work without being dependent on external rewards like money, power, or fame. A fortune will always be relative to the person who has more, and fame is fleeting. While you may be rewarded with a large bonus or major recognition at certain times, most days consist of making a little forward progress without external reward. This is why identifying meaning and purpose in the process of your daily work is essential.

Whenever possible, get your motivation from doing things that contribute to a collective good. Incentives based on group performance have been shown to boost innovation more than individual incentives. Instead of focusing solely on your own performance at work, find a way to gauge the performance of your team. Then put your energy into helping the group achieve. Working toward a shared mission with other people will add a positive charge to each day.

5

Ask What the World Needs

When the Great Recession hit in 2008, Ron Finley's fashion business was ruined. But Finley found another way to apply his creative talents. Driving the streets around his Compton home, Finley realized that his neighborhood was profoundly unhealthy. There were countless fast food restaurants and dialysis centers in South Central Los Angeles — but there were no gardens, and access to fresh fruits and vegetables was limited.

Finley redirected his creative energy to address this need. He planted fruits and vegetables in abandoned lots, outside his home, and on traffic medians. Between the sidewalk and the street near Finley's home, you can now see an explosion of green, punctuated with color. There are sunflowers, a banana tree, blackberries, raspberries, a pomegranate tree, an apple tree, a plum tree, a fig tree, an almond tree, squash, lemongrass, rosemary, and a host of other plants.

"It's all art," he says. "With this art, you build community. You build your health, you build lasting relationships, because you can trade food." He wanted to show his community that anyone could grow their own food, and at the same time surround themself with beauty.

You create meaning when your strengths and interests meet the needs of the world. Knowing your talents and passions is critical, but that is only half of this supply-and-demand equation. What may be even more important is understanding what the world needs from you and how you can productively apply your strengths and interests.

Start with a focus on others' needs to ensure that the things you are passionate about have a practical application. Finding a way to make a difference through your work requires the same kind of analysis that businesses perform when designing new products. Just as a company would not invest millions in a product that wouldn't serve many customers, you don't want to invest thousands of hours developing a talent or interest when there is little demand for it from your employer or your community.

One of the rightful critiques of all the "follow your passion" advice is that it presumes that you are the center of the world, and pursuing your own joy is the objective of life. Those who make a profound difference, in contrast, begin by asking *what they can give*. Starting with this question allows you to direct your talents toward what matters most for others.

Step back for a moment and explore some of the most pressing needs in your social circles, organization, or community. Look for specific problems or issues that require time and attention. As you think about what people around you need most, identify areas that overlap with your strengths and interests.

Maybe a company needs a talented graphic designer, a child needs a mentor, or a community group needs someone with expertise in fundraising. Look for ways that your unique talents, background, expertise, dreams, and desires can serve some of these local and global needs. What is your unique purpose that continually sets you apart from your peers? What do you believe in so deeply that you're willing to sacrifice short-term happiness in order to make it happen?

Double Down on Your Talents

There is something that you can do better than anyone else in the world. You were born with talents as unique as your DNA. Perhaps you have noticed how some people have a natural ability to comfort others in times of need. Another person has an innate curiosity and is always learning. And the next person has a great deal of talent for selling and persuading. These differences create far more diversity than broad categories of gender, race, age, or nationality do. This diversity of talent is what makes individuals distinct from one another.

Yet society keeps telling you that you can be anything you want to be . . . if you just try hard enough. This age-old aspirational myth does more harm than good. While people can overcome adversity and are remarkably resilient, the most potential for growth and development lies in the areas where you have natural talent to start with. The more time you spend building on who you already are, the faster you will grow.

That is the main lesson I learned from my late mentor and grandfather, Don Clifton, who spent a lifetime studying people's strengths. Instead of aspiring to be anything you want to be, you should aim to be more of who you already are. Starting with your natural talents — then investing time in practicing, building skills, and increasing knowledge — yields a much greater return.

Gallup's research suggests that when you use your strengths, you can *double your number of high-quality work hours* per week from 20 to 40. It also reveals that people who focus on their strengths every day are six times as likely to be engaged in their jobs and more than three times as likely to have high levels of overall life satisfaction.

If you spend most of your life trying to be good at everything, you eliminate your chances of being *great* at anything. Unless your goal is to be mediocre at a lot of things, starting with what you are naturally good at is a matter of efficiency. Focusing on strengths is in many ways a basic time-allocation issue. Every hour you invest in an area where you have natural talent has a multiplying effect, whereas each hour you spend trying to remedy a weakness is like working against a gravitational force. Yet many people spend years or even decades working on weaknesses in hopes that doing so will make them well-rounded.

Do everything you can to avoid falling into this trap. While well-roundedness may be helpful for acquiring the basic tools for any trade — such as reading, writing, and arithmetic — it loses value as you get closer to finding a career. At that point, what's more important and relevant is what sets you apart. If you want to be great at something in your lifetime, double down on your talents at every turn.

Act Now Before Today Is Gone

Throughout my career, I have underestimated the importance of being interested in the work you do every day. Until a couple of years ago, much of the research I had read, primarily from studies on hiring people for entry-level jobs, did not find a very strong relationship between job applicants' personal interests and their subsequent performance at work. However, recent studies and experiments have changed my perspective on this topic.

A 2012 study found that when interest profiles match specific job profiles, performance, relationships on the job, and likelihood to stay with the organization improve. Another series of experiments, published in 2014 by a team from Duke, helps explain why interest is critical to success. As you might expect, when people were assigned tasks that matched their interests, they performed better. This happens because activity that is personally interesting "creates an energized experience that allows people to persist when persisting would otherwise cause them to burn out," according to one of the study's authors.

But how much of your time in a typical day is dedicated to activities that *give you a positive charge or make a long-term contribution to society*? When researchers ask people to keep a journal of how they spend their day, it is remarkable how little time falls into either of these meaningful pursuits that create sustainable well-being.

The reality is, you don't always have tomorrow to do what matters most. A couple of years ago, I wrestled with this thought extensively, given my health challenges and interest in this topic. Consequently, I stepped away from a workplace consulting job so I could spend all of my time on research and writing about how to improve health. I felt like I *had* to do something to help countless friends and loved ones who were battling heart disease, cancer, diabetes, and obesity. When I asked myself how I could use my strengths and interests to do more for the people I care about, it took me in a new direction.

If you fail to do meaningful work that makes a difference today, the day is gone forever. You can try to make up for it tomorrow, but most likely you won't. Before you know it, several days will have gone by, then a few years. A decade later, you may look back and realize that you missed the opportunity to contribute to the growth of another person, pursue a new interest, or launch a new product. But the opportunity to do something you love will always be there, as long as you start *today*.

6

Don't Fall Into the Default

Even when people think they are chasing their lifelong ambitions, in many cases, they are following the dreams of someone they admire. Consider how many people you know who have followed in the footsteps of a sibling, parent, or mentor at some point in their career. If you think about the way many people are raised — surrounded by role models and examples — the carryover of one generation's aspirations to the next makes perfect sense.

Many of my friends from college went on to attend law school, mainly because of families or cultures that pushed them in that direction. Other friends pursued a graduate degree in law primarily for salary and security. Only one of my close friends went to law school because he had an extraordinary amount of talent and passion in that area.

A couple of decades later, he is the only one I know who continues to practice law.

A Canadian study of more than 71,000 pairs of fathers and sons published in the *Journal of Labor Economics* reveals just how likely people are to gravitate toward a parent's career choice. Longitudinal research into young men's career choices over decades, starting in 1963, found that about 40 percent went on to work for the *same employer* as their father at some point in their career. Even more striking was the fact that nearly 70 percent of boys who had fathers in the top income bracket went to work for the same company. It is important to note that this large-scale study was limited to men, given the makeup of the workforce during the 1960s. However, smaller studies suggest that a mother's occupational choices have an even more direct influence than a father's choices on a daughter's career choice.

It is perfectly normal for proud parents to want to share the things they have learned with a son or daughter. And it's certainly not a bad thing to follow in a parent's footsteps. You learn a great deal from the people you spend time with growing up, and often interests and passions converge. However, this puts an additional responsibility on you — to ensure that you are following *your own* dreams.

Cast a Shadow Instead of Living in One

When I am out for an evening walk with my five-year-old daughter and three-year-old son, we often play games with our shadows on the street as the sun sets. If either of my children walks into the path of my much larger shadow, their image disappears. When my son steps into his big sister's shadow, he has to move a bit faster to escape. What my kids love most is being able to see their full image projected on the street ahead, which grows in size as the sun sets in the background.

While we have fun with this, I can't help but think about what this imagery represents. For me, it is a great reminder of the basic human need to carve out one's own image. As a parent, I need to avoid the temptation and ease of treating my children the same. I have to avoid pressuring them into boxes created by society's expectations or my own. My role is to help my children be more of who they already are.

I can spot early traces of unique talent in my children, even at their young ages. My three-year-old son is remarkably observant and inquisitive. Simply telling him to do something because "it's a rule" is typically met with a defiant "no." Instead, he learns by observing *why*. His five-year-old sister, in contrast, loves structure and teaching people about what she has learned. She also has an unusual ability to remember things and has a natural gift for empathizing with and relating to people.

As my children grow up, I have no doubt that both subtle and overt pressures will steer them in different directions. It is already tempting for me to imagine my daughter being a great teacher, like her mother, or a smart and caring physician. Given schools' intense focus on science, technology, education, and math, I'm sure that both my son and my daughter will feel pressure to excel in these subjects. Yet when they enter the work world, the most valuable goal they can have will be to do something that provides a positive charge and creates meaning.

Everyone grows up with different expectations. One of the best ways to find your areas of interest or passion is by exploring new subjects. If a parent, friend, or mentor introduces you to something you enjoy that builds on your natural talents, it can be quite informative. There is nothing better than working on something you love with people you love. However, it is also easy to fall into a "default career path" — one that is more about other people's expectations than about your internal motivations.

The only shadow you should live in is your own. You were born with unique traits and influenced by people who helped you become what you are today. To do justice to those who have invested in you, the challenge is to live the life you want.

Craft Your Dream Into Your Job

Every day you let something keep you from following a dream, you lose an opportunity to create meaning. However, few people find their ideal job on their first attempt. This is why chipping away at a dream in small steps can be deeply motivating.

You should be able to spend *some* time every day engaging in activities that energize and recharge you. This is an important distinction; it takes only a few moments to make a day more productive and fulfilling. Even in the worst situations, you can find opportunities for growth. The key is to shift your focus away from what others do that hinders you — or from work situations beyond your control — and instead seek out small things that enable you to make daily forward progress. You can always do something to boost the spirits of a colleague or customer, despite what is going on in other areas of your work.

Even if you are stuck in a job that is far from ideal, you have the ability to create a little meaning on the side. Volunteering in your community is a great way to spend meaningful time every month. I have several friends who say they get more personal satisfaction from a few hours of volunteering than they do from anything else. This can also be a great way to explore new areas and interests that may turn into something larger down the road.

A new body of research suggests that people forge great jobs with effort, as opposed to finding them through job postings. This research, led by a team at the University of Michigan, found that you can craft existing jobs to significantly improve the meaningfulness of your work. Effective "job crafting" starts by looking at how much time you dedicate to specific *tasks* that give you energy each day. It also entails looking at the way your *relationships* at work and your *perception* of what you do create meaning for others. If you review these three areas, you should be able to build some of your dreams into your current job.

Think back through your education and career. Identify a few instances when you felt such a positive charge that you lost track of time. Make note of exactly what you were doing and who you were with at these times. Then see if you can bring that into your current work and think about one thing you can do tomorrow to spend more time in your element.

Also consider how you can spend more time around specific people who energize your work and less time around those who don't. You can do more for other people if you stay clear of those who consistently stress you out or drag you down. Work is like any other social network: both negative and positive emotions spread quickly.

7

Initiate to Shape the Future

In this age of infinite information and endless distraction, it's easy to spend an entire day reacting and responding. Demands coming at you from others will always consume some portion of your day. Yet in most cases, what you will be most proud of a decade from now will not be anything that was a result of you simply responding.

What will matter later in life is what you *initiate* today — striking up a conversation that leads to a new friendship, sharing an idea with someone at work that turns into a new product or offering, or investing in another person's growth and watching her succeed over the years. If you want to create a positive charge for others, your ability to do so will be almost directly proportional to the amount of time you can spend initiating instead of responding.

Yet it's much easier to react and respond to what others want. Do a quick calculation of the percentage of time you spend responding to things in a typical day (answering email and phone calls, etc.). Compare this with the percentage of time you spend initiating actions. In most cases, reactionary time greatly outweighs proactive time. When you're having trouble at work or feeling stuck, that is the best time to bring your focus back to what you can do to change the situation.

While some people feel like their job *is* to respond, in most cases, it is not. If you work in a role serving customers directly and answer their questions with the minimal amount of information required, you could have a day full of responding. This approach is not good for you, your organization, or your customers. However, if you individualize your interaction with each person, anticipate a future need, or help even more than a customer expects, that *is* initiating.

Manage your communications, online and offline, instead of letting them run your life. If you don't, you will inadvertently spend a majority of your time responding to other people's needs instead of creating anything that lasts. While you can't predict what will happen in the future, by initiating something new each day, you will be a part of creating that future.

Put Purpose Before Busyness

Being "busy" is often the antithesis of working on what matters most. Yet when I ask friends or colleagues how they are doing, some variant of "I'm busy" is the most common response I receive. What's worse, for more than a decade, "I'm busy" has been my standard response when people ask me how I am doing.

Like many others, I have been caught in the trap of mistaking activity for real progress. If a mouse runs on a wheel for 12 hours in a row, it will have been "very busy" the entire day, yet it will have gone nowhere and achieved nothing.

Similarly, on many days, I confused busyness with meaningful progress. I would boast that I had worked my way through more than 200 emails or sat through eight hours of important meetings. Most of the time, I was multitasking and doing both — responding to emails while using a headset to participate in conference calls.

I started to notice a similar pattern in most workplaces. Employees feel the need to look, act, and talk as if they are so busy that a gaping hole would appear in the universe if they missed a day of work. In their minds, this shows others how hard they work and how essential they are to the organization.

You can't blame anyone for learning to equate busyness with importance, given the way it is built into social expectations. However, the result of trying to be busy is a poorly managed life. If you are busy throughout the day and bouncing from one thing to the next, you're probably not focusing on constructive activity. You are also probably not giving your full attention to the things that matter most, from working to spending time with your family.

Instead, aim for a daily routine that allows you enough time to do what you want, work on projects that make a difference, and spend time with people who matter to you. I have started forcing myself to substitute thinking "I'm busy" with "I need to do a better job managing my time." That little mental trick helps me prioritize. Whether you try this or something else, find a better answer than being busy all the time. Work smarter, not harder.

Focus on Less to Do More

Staying connected is now remarkably easy. As a result, getting anything of substance done is not. The average American, for example, spends eight and a half hours in front of a screen and receives a whopping 63,000 words of new information each day. When workers sit in front of a computer screen, no more than three minutes at a time go by without interruption.

A study of 150,000 smartphone users found that these devices are unlocked *110 times per day* on average. During peak evening hours, people check their devices nine times an hour. From email and text messages to breaking news alerts, phone calls, and social network updates, distraction is the new default. By one estimate, the average worker loses 28 percent of each day to distraction. Only one in five workers report having the ability to focus on one thing at a time during a workday.

On average, people spend about half of their time thinking about something other than what they are doing at any given moment. According to one very detailed study by Harvard's Matt Killingsworth and Dan Gilbert, people reported that their minds were wandering 47 percent of the time. What's even more disturbing is that this is not *pleasant* mind wandering; instead, the distractedness tends to make them less happy.

Killingsworth and Gilbert wrote, "A human mind is a wandering mind, and a wandering mind is an unhappy mind." During almost all of the activities they studied — walking, eating, talking to a colleague, shopping, watching television — people spend no less than 30 percent of the time with their minds wandering. There's even a very good chance that your mind is wandering while you are reading this book.

Trying to do a little bit of everything leads to doing nothing of substance. When you let the demands of a day pull you in 20 different directions, they do exactly that — causing you to react to a bunch of small things instead of doing anything big. Working while distracted has also been shown to decrease performance and quality levels. In most cases, the human mind simply functions better when it is highly focused.

Saying no to distractions can be challenging. But it is something you need to do for the sake of focusing on the things that matter most. The rare occasions when I have been able to completely disconnect for a full day of writing have been some of the most peaceful, productive, and liberating days of my life. And oddly enough, everything around me continues to go smoothly, without missing a beat.

If you can eliminate a few small distractions that take up a great deal of your time, then you can spend more time on things that energize you and give you a positive charge. This additional mental downtime can also help you be more creative. Start by writing down one thing you are doing today that you know is not a good use of your time. Commit to changing your pattern to do less of it. Then come up with a short list of distracting things you will do less of in the future.

The next time a new opportunity presents itself, think carefully before you make an ongoing commitment. If it is something you feel you should take on, determine what other activity you might need to let go of. When you are struggling between two choices, remember that there is always a third option: doing nothing. In many cases, declining both options is the best route.

Silence Pavlov's Bell

In the late 1800s, Russian physiologist Ivan Pavlov first observed that dogs could be conditioned to start salivating the moment they heard a bell ring. He had taught the dogs to associate the bell with receiving their food; thus, the dogs drooled in expectation every time they heard the bell ring. This phenomenon came to be known as "classical conditioning," and it is exactly what you do every time you hear a buzzing that indicates you have a new message.

Each time your computer dings to signal a new email, your phone vibrates with a new text message, or you see a notification on your screen, you associate these stimuli with the "reward" of having new information available to read. A few decades ago, all of your mail arrived just once a day, when it was delivered to your physical mailbox. This system provided structure: you could count on receiving a batch of information at roughly the same time each day and could then consume it all at once. Today, endless notifications have turned into the electronic equivalent of Pavlov's bell.

Most job descriptions do not list checking email and social networking sites as a core part of anyone's daily responsibilities. Yet people often spend more time on these activities than they do on more productive investments of their working time. One study estimated that professionals spend at least half of their day responding to email and checking social networks.

The most disturbing finding from this study is the degree to which people allow messages to interrupt their work. Nearly a quarter of workers basically sit around watching their inboxes, and read information the second it arrives. Another 43 percent admit to checking messages more than they should. Only 30 percent of people check their messages occasionally, but not to an excessive degree. This means that more than two-thirds of people could be letting electronic communications run their lives, causing undue anxiety.

A 2015 study from the University of British Columbia found that people experience less stress if they check their email fewer times a day. Yet many continue to experience what researchers dubbed "telepressure," or feeling the need to respond immediately. When people experience telepressure, it is associated with a decrease in sleep quality, more sick days, and the likelihood of mental and physical burnout.

To overcome some of the most common distractions, shut off the alerts that break into your day every few minutes. Email and phone calls are the two most common disturbances that infringe on people's time, according to a recent survey. Other interrupters include toggling between applications, checking social network feeds, instant messaging, text messaging, and Web searching.

I have found that even something as subtle as glancing at a "breaking news" notification on my smartphone's lock screen can ruin my concentration. It seems like most of the messages and notifications are from people or organizations who think it is important that you see their messages immediately. This is why halting these alerts, even for short blocks of time, can do wonders. One group estimates that it takes 67 seconds to recover from every message you read.

Most of these alerts are easy to turn off when you want to get things done. Almost every phone has a ringer switch. Messaging programs allow you to turn off instant notifications. Perhaps acknowledging the magnitude of this problem, the newest smartphones include a "do not disturb" setting that prevents all (non-emergency) calls, messages, and notifications from interrupting you.

Take a moment today to tweak your routine to minimize interruption. Set specific times to catch up on news, email, and social networking sites. Keep distractions from buzzing, dinging, vibrating, and flying through your visual field whenever you need to focus on important work or pay attention to other people. It's fine to check your messages, just don't let them chase you around all day.

Focus for 45, Break for 15

While I was working on this book, I stumbled across an article written by Tim Walker, an American school-teacher who moved to Finland in 2014 and began teaching fifth grade at a public school in Helsinki. What grabbed my attention was his skepticism about a nuance of the Finnish educational system.

In Finland, for every 45 minutes in the classroom, students are given a 15-minute break. At first, Walker resisted following this routine and instead kept his students in the classroom. But he eventually decided to test the 45/15 model, and he was astounded by the result. Walker described how kids were no longer dragging their feet in a "zombie-like" state. Instead, they walked into the room with a renewed bounce in their step after each 15-minute break, and they were more focused on learning throughout the day. The more Walker studied this model, which has been in place in Finland since the 1960s, he discovered that it wasn't about what students did during this break time; instead, simply giving them freedom from structured work gave them renewed energy and focus.

More formal experiments on this topic have found that students are consistently more attentive in class when they have regular breaks. The research also suggests that it is important that these breaks consist of free time, as opposed to activities structured by teachers.

Reading Tim Walker's story made me wonder if a similar hourly structure could be beneficial for adults as well. The answer to this question may lie in DeskTime, a software application that meticulously tracks employees' time use throughout the day. When the makers of this software looked at the most productive 10 percent of their 36,000-employee user base, they made some surprising discoveries. What the most productive people have in common is an ability to take effective breaks. These elite 10 percent work for 52 minutes at a time, then take a 17-minute break before diving back into their work.

According to Julia Gifford, who works with DeskTime and wrote the report, the reason this pattern helps productivity is that the top 10 percent treat the periods of working time like a sprint. "They make the most of those 52 minutes by working with intense purpose, but then rest up to be ready for the next burst," Gifford wrote. She also noted that during the 17 minutes of break, the group was more likely to go for a walk or tune out rather than checking email or Facebook.

While the ideal ratios will vary by profession and occupation, there is a great deal of support for the general notion of working in intense bursts paired with a period of time to recharge. If it is practical for you, try working in highly focused bursts of about 45 minutes, and then take a 15-minute break. Adjust up or down from there to determine what ratio allows you to remain fully charged throughout the workday. Even carving out 5 or 10 minutes for a break should help. In Gifford's words, short breaks that get you ready for each sprint are the essence of "work with purpose."

Use Purpose to Prevent Plaque

Serving a higher purpose can prevent mental deterioration and Alzheimer's disease later in life. It can also help you think better and sharpen your mental acuity. At least, that's what researchers at Rush University Medical Center found when they studied a group of people as they aged for a decade.

To look at the effect on the brain of having a purpose in life, this team of scientists followed 246 participants who subsequently died. For up to 10 years, the participants were given annual clinical evaluations, which included detailed cognitive testing and neurological exams. They also answered questions about their purpose in life and how they derived meaning from life's experiences. Then, after the subjects passed away, the scientists conducted autopsies of each person's brain and quantified the amount of brain plaques and tangles. These plaques and tangles disrupt memory and other cognitive functions and are very common among people who develop Alzheimer's.

Dr. Patricia Boyle, one of the study's authors, stated, "These findings suggest that purpose in life protects against the harmful effects of plaques and tangles on memory and other thinking abilities. This is encouraging and suggests that engaging in meaningful and purposeful activities promotes cognitive health in old age."

Being able to see the purpose of your work also yields benefits for your health and well-being. A 14-year study of more than 6,000 people found that those with a sense of purpose had a 15 percent lower risk of death. What's more, the research found that this longevity benefit is not dependent on age. So, whether you are 20, 40, or 60, being able to see the purpose of your work gives you a long-term advantage.

Keep Your Mission in Mind

Try to remind yourself why you do what you do every day. Bringing your mission to the forefront keeps you motivated. It could also make you a lot more productive.

Consider what happened when Wharton School of Business professor Adam Grant first studied the motivation of call center workers who spent their days calling the school's alumni to request donations for future scholarship recipients. Given the job's degree of difficulty (calling people in the evening and asking them for money) and its high level of turnover, Grant wondered if introducing call center workers to an actual scholarship recipient would provide additional motivation. So Grant and his fellow researchers brought in a scholarship recipient to speak with one group of these workers for a mere five minutes.

A month later, the call center workers who had spoken with the scholarship recipient were remarkably more productive. This group made almost twice as many calls per hour. Before the intervention, each caller raised about $400 per week; afterward, they raised about $2,000 per week.

Since this original research more than a decade ago, Adam Grant has studied these "pro-social" tendencies in several environments. In a technology company's call center, for example, hearing from internal colleagues who benefited from their work was more meaningful to employees than motivating words from the organization's CEO. In hospitals, Grant and his colleagues found that signs reading HAND HYGIENE PREVENTS *YOU* FROM CATCHING DISEASES had no effect, yet signs reading HAND HYGIENE PREVENTS *PATIENTS* FROM CATCHING DISEASES increased use of soap and hand sanitizer by 45 percent among doctors and nurses.

If, in your job, you have difficulty seeing the direct influence you have on another person, it's worth taking the time to try to make that connection. General Electric is aware of the value of making this connection. The company brings cancer survivors to visit the men and women who build the large mechanical scanners (MRIs) that help people track and prevent cancer. GE's videos from these events illuminate how much meaning and purpose everyone on the manufacturing floor experiences upon seeing the very real (and emotional) impact of their work.

As part of one experiment, patient photos were included when radiologists reviewed CT or MRI scans. In most cases, radiologists simply looked at scans and did not see or meet the actual patient. However, when a photograph was included, the radiologists admitted feeling more empathy toward the patient, and they wrote 29 percent longer reports. Most important, when a photo was attached, the radiologists' accuracy of diagnosis improved by 46 percent.

Other organizations coordinate regular "field trips" so employees who do not typically see the results of their work can make that connection. John Deere invites employees who build tractors to spend time with the farmers who use the company's products. Wells Fargo shows its bankers videos of people describing how low-interest loans saved them from severe debt. Facebook invites software developers to hear from people who made connections with long-lost friends and family members through its vast social network.

Find a way to infuse each day with a reminder of your mission. It can be as simple as keeping a story of the impact of your work on hand or having an image, quote, or statement that brings the "why" of your job to life. If you want to stay motivated about the contribution you make to society, keep the mission at the forefront of your mind.

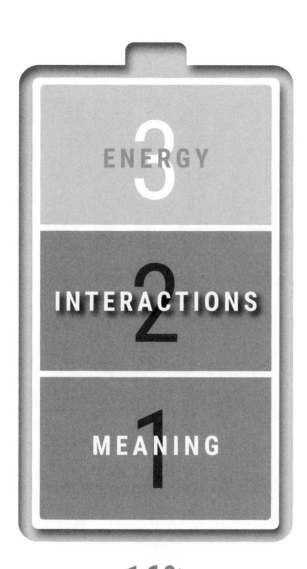

16%
of people had extremely
positive interactions yesterday

Make Every Interaction Count

As a young internist on Chicago's South Side in the 1990s, Dr. Nicholas Christakis would take his leather medical bag and make house calls on the dying. As he visited his patients, a mix of working class African Americans and University of Chicago faculty members, Christakis had a unique view of the impact of dying and death on loved ones. This led him to study the widowhood effect, a phenomenon also referred to as a spouse dying of a broken heart.

The doctor's perspective was forever changed one day when he received a call on his cell phone. Christakis had just been visiting an elderly woman, dying of dementia, who was being cared for by her daughter. As he was leaving her house, Christakis answered the phone and heard a voice on the line he did not recognize.

The caller turned out to be the *best friend of the daughter's husband*. Caring for her mother left the daughter exhausted, and the daughter's exhaustion had left her husband sick. The man was calling because he was concerned about his best friend. In that moment, Christakis realized the widowhood effect didn't just affect one person but an entire network of people.

He has since gone on to study how networks of relationships affect everything from obesity and smoking to voting and how nice you are. Through the elaborate mapping of relationships and behaviors over time, Christakis and his colleagues have shown that we are not only influenced by interactions with our friends but also by our friends' friends — and our friends' friends' friends. People we've never even met.

Each of our interactions also ripples outward in the network. "When you lose weight, when you act happy, when you act kindly . . . you affect other people and they in turn affect other people. And by our estimates you can affect ten, a hundred, sometimes more, individuals from your actions," says Christakis, now a professor and co-director of the Yale Institute for Network Science.

Life is a composite of millions of individual interactions. These moments — which usually involve an exchange with another person — give your days a positive or negative charge. The actions you take throughout every single day accumulate to shape your years, decades, and overall life. However, when you think about a typical day, it's easy to take these moments for granted.

Even brief interactions count, such as exchanging a smile or greeting while passing someone on the street. If you look at moments as three-second windows, there are 1,200 moments per hour and 19,200 in a day. That equates to roughly 500 million moments over a lifetime. The frequency of these brief experiences, within a given day, is far more important than their intensity, as research on this topic confirms.

For example, a person who has a dozen mildly positive things happen during a day will feel better than someone who has one single truly amazing thing happen. Even in a single day, it is the little things that count. My team's research found that people who reported having great interactions throughout the day were *nearly four times* as likely to have very high well-being.

Of course, there are many life-altering events that you cannot change, no matter how hard you try. But you absolutely can control your next interaction with another person. No matter how bad of a mood you are in, you can make a conscious choice to add a positive spin to your next conversation. If you do, it is likely to improve your subsequent interactions. It should also set off a positive charge in the other person, resulting in additional energy for your overall environment.

Assume Good Intent

With each interaction comes a choice. When you run into someone who is filled with rage or hostility or who flat-out ignores you, that negativity can cancel out any positive exchanges that might have followed.

Let's say you are standing outside a coffee shop talking to friends when a guy walks by in a hurry and bumps you, causing you to spill your coffee. In this moment, it is crucial to do everything you can to turn this mishap into a positive situation, even if the other person is at fault and nowhere nearly as apologetic as he should be. Especially when you are dealing with a stranger, there is no way you can put yourself precisely in his shoes.

In many cases, I am the one accidentally bumping into other people. As I mentioned in the first chapter, I lost all vision in my left eye to cancer many years ago. I now wear a prosthetic shell, which looks almost identical to my good eye. As a result, when someone approaches me from the left side, they think I see them . . . but I don't.

Each time my partial blindness leads to a collision, it gives me a little window into what's going on in the other person's life at that moment. Most people follow my (well-rehearsed) lead of smiling, apologizing profusely, and shaking it off. However, some people are quick to assign blame and express clear agitation through their voice and body language.

It didn't take me long to realize that the other person's reaction is more important for *their* subsequent well-being than it is for mine. Those who assume bad intent are doing a disservice to themselves. As Pepsico CEO Indra Nooyi described it, "When you assume negative intent, you're angry. If you take away that anger and assume positive intent, you will be amazed . . . [You] don't get defensive. You don't scream. You are trying to understand and listen."

Even when faced with obvious bad intent — which is rare — it is still in your best interest to try to turn the situation into something positive. Then you avoid getting worked up and dwelling on it for the rest of the day. As you go through each day interacting with friends and strangers, make it your mission to ensure that as many exchanges as possible turn out a little bit better than they started.

Focus on the Frequency

All relationships are formed through a series of interactions. If you meet someone new today and have a negative experience with that person, you are less likely to seek him out in the future. If you have a positive exchange, you have a much better chance of building a healthy relationship. This part of the equation is pretty obvious. What many people take for granted is that *existing* relationships require regular and frequent interactions to thrive.

As Nicholas Christakis first discovered in the 1990s, the people you interact with throughout the day have an enormous influence on your well-being. In 2008, when Christakis and his colleague James Fowler studied the way relationships affect happiness levels, *physical proximity* mattered much more than I would have guessed. If a friend in one of the participants' social networks lived within half a mile of that participant (and was happy), the probability of the participant's happiness increased by more than 40 percent.

If a friend in someone's network lived within two miles of the participant, this influence was cut in half to about 20 percent. When a friend in a participant's social network lived more than three miles away, the effect went down to about 10 percent. This influence continued to decrease with additional distance. Christakis and Fowler noted, "The spread of happiness might depend more on frequent social contact than deep social connections."

That being said, close relationships can have a profound effect over time, even when those in the relationship live in a different city or country. It is certainly worth investing time in maintaining and nurturing distant connections — an undertaking that is now much easier thanks to technology and social networks.

A controversial 2013 study conducted by a team of Princeton researchers found what they described as "massive-scale emotional contagion through networks." To test whether emotions spread through brief online inter-actions, the researchers altered the Facebook news feed of 689,003 users (this was the controversial part of the study, as it was not clear whether these users had opted into an experiment). When positive expressions in the news feed were deliberately reduced, people generated fewer positive posts and instead wrote more negative posts. When negative expressions were deliberately reduced, the opposite occurred, and users were more positive in their subsequent posts.

All of this research makes it clear that people greatly underestimate how everyday interactions influence their daily experience. Everyone you communicate with on a daily or weekly basis, whether you consider them friends or even know their name, influences your well-being. This also means that you have the ability to add a positive charge to every conversation throughout your day.

10

Be 80 Percent Positive

When someone is positive all the time, I often struggle to wrestle the conversation into reality. Being blindly positive has more in common with perpetual negativity than I would have guessed. Both conditions cause others to be frustrated or annoyed or to simply tune out.

This is why some of the best research on daily experience is rooted in *ratios* of positive and negative interactions. Over the last two decades, scientists have made remarkable predictions simply by watching people interact with one another and then scoring the conversations based on the ratio of positive and negative interactions. Researchers have used the findings to predict everything from the likelihood a couple will divorce to the odds of a work team having high customer satisfaction and productivity levels.

More recent research helps explain why these brief exchanges matter so much. When you experience negative emotions as a result of criticism or rejection, for example, your body produces higher levels of the stress hormone cortisol, which shuts down much of your thinking and activates conflict and defense mechanisms. You perceive situations as being worse than they actually are when you are in this fight-or-flight mode. The release of cortisol is also a sustained response, so it lasts for a while, especially if you dwell on the negative event.

When you experience a positive interaction, it activates a very different response. Positive exchanges boost your body's production of oxytocin, a feel-good hormone that increases your ability to communicate, collaborate, and trust others. When oxytocin activates networks in your prefrontal cortex, it leads to more expansive thought and action. However, oxytocin metabolizes faster than cortisol, so the effects of a positive surge are less dramatic and enduring than they are for a negative one.

We need at least three to five positive interactions to outweigh every one negative exchange. Bad moments simply outweigh good ones. Whether you're having a one-on-one conversation with a colleague or a group discussion, keep this simple shortcut in mind: *At least 80 percent of your conversations should be focused on what's going right.*

Workplaces, for example, often have this backward. During performance reviews, managers routinely spend 80 percent of their time on weaknesses, gaps, and "areas for improvement." They spend roughly 20 percent of the time on strengths and positive aspects. They need to flip this around. Any time you have discussions with a team or group, spend the vast majority of the time talking about *what is working*, and use the remaining time to address deficits.

Use Positive Words as Glue

Most of the words you use carry either a positive charge or a negative charge. Fortunately, there is what researchers call a "positive bias in human expression." The vast majority of words people use are more positive than negative. In large-scale studies on this topic spanning multiple countries, roughly four out of every five words used in writing were found to be positive.

Positive words, whether used verbally or in writing, are the glue that holds relationships together. Most conversations, letters, and emails are overwhelmingly positive. They need to be so the heavily weighted negative words do not counteract them.

Words with a negative charge have roughly four times the weight of those with a positive charge. If you type a note to a friend and make one negative remark, it will take approximately four positive comments just to get that person back to neutral. If you have an online debate with a colleague, every sentence the recipient perceives as negative will increase the deficit.

When you need to challenge someone, address difficult issues, or deliver bad news, just be sure to mention a few positive things as well. Balance the overall conversation with far more positive than negative words. Then try to close with specific and hopeful actions. Help the other person see the positive consequences of any changes you discuss. If you bombard the recipient with negative remarks, which have a disproportionate influence, he is more likely to shut down and not listen.

Teachers, for example, are often told to structure parent-teacher conferences with this idea in mind. When conferences start on a good note, parents are more likely to listen and be receptive.

Any time you are communicating with another person, be mindful of the importance of using positive words to hold things together. It may seem inconsequential in the moment, but subtle messages stick in a person's mind. If friends know they can count on a message or phone call from you to boost their mood a little, it will strengthen the bonds of your relationships.

At Least Pay Attention

Even when you can't say something nice, go ahead and say something. Contrary to what I was told growing up, negative comments are less harmful than ignoring someone. A study conducted by Canadian researchers in 2014 suggests that being ignored at work is even more detrimental to mental and physical well-being than harassment or bullying.

As one of the study's co-authors put it, "We've been taught that ignoring someone is socially preferable . . . but ostracism actually leads people to feel more helpless, like they're not worthy of any attention at all." Participants in this study rated ignoring someone as being the safer and less detrimental route, even though it did more damage. People who were ostracized in the workplace had less engagement with their work, were more likely to leave their job, and had more health problems compared with workers who reported they had been bullied.

While the comparison to bullying in this study is dramatic, the overall finding is consistent with a great deal of research I have studied and conducted. Having a manager who is not paying attention nearly doubles your odds of being disengaged on the job compared with a manager who focuses primarily on your weaknesses.

People commonly underestimate the value of simply paying attention to another person. When people are ignored, they have a tendency to assume the worst. If someone I communicate with regularly has not spoken to me in some time, I am quick to wonder if I did something wrong or offended them. Most of the time, this is not the case. But the brain often perceives a lack of communication as something much worse.

Even negative feedback is better than nothing at all. When others critique you, at least you know they care enough to pay attention. The ideal scenario is when a dose of reality is paired with several servings of encouragement.

11

Start Small and Be Clear

If you allow society to keep redefining happiness for you, you'll enter a race that you have no chance of winning. Everywhere you turn, something is suggesting that you need more to find true contentment and satisfaction in life. To persuade you to consume more than you have today, marketers will continue to make a case for why you will be happier if you can just get to the top of the next hill. But getting caught up in this race only ensures that you'll never win.

Fortunately, the things that give your day a positive charge are usually in plain sight and do not require major purchases. A warm interaction with your spouse on your way out. Stopping by a colleague's desk to share a few words of praise. Going for walk outside on a nice day. Talking to one of your best friends on the phone and giving her the gift of your attention when she needs it most.

These small gestures might even be more effective at boosting another person's well-being than larger acts, according to a recent study from Stanford and Harvard Business School. As part of a series of experiments, one group of participants was assigned a goal of making another person happy, while a second group was told to simply do something that made another person smile. The results showed that small, straightforward actions to make someone smile were far more effective than broad, nebulous attempts to improve overall happiness.

The study's authors wrote, "Acts with small, concrete goals designed to improve the well-being of others are more likely to lead to happiness for the giver than are acts with large, abstract goals — despite people's intuitions to the contrary." This study reveals a surprisingly simple way to approach major challenges. When a friend is going through a difficult time, do something to lift her spirits before you get into the bigger issues.

Use Questions to Spark Conversation

Whether you struggle to strike up a conversation or it comes naturally, you will benefit from talking to new people. I understand how challenging it can be to initiate a conversation with someone you don't know in a room full of people. In fact, the mere thought of it increases my heart rate. Yet I have learned that it's easier to start talking with people when I focus on asking good questions and then listen to the answers. Asking questions reduces my social anxiety because I no longer feel the need to say something interesting to join a conversation or fit in. While trying to win people over is not a strength of mine, I love observing and learning about interesting people.

Asking questions is even more effective when others may be skeptical of your influence or credibility or when you are engaged in a debate. A team of researchers in the United Kingdom who have been studying recordings of expert negotiators for many years found that questions are one of the most effective forms of bringing people into agreement. The average negotiators spent less than 10 percent of their total time asking questions during a given session. However, the most successful group of negotiators spent 21 percent of their time asking questions.

People love to talk about themselves. By some estimates, 40 percent of everyday speech consists of people telling others what they think and feel. According to scientists, talking about oneself triggers the same reward centers in the brain as food or money. Diana Tamir, a Harvard neuroscientist who conducted experiments that included brain imaging on this topic explained, "Self-disclosure is extra rewarding . . . [P]eople were even willing to forgo money in order to talk about themselves."

The more open you are about yourself, including revealing embarrassing moments and occasional mistakes, the more likely another person is to trust you. So accept your own small mistakes, slip-ups, and natural quirks. A series of experiments suggests that being humble and embracing self-deprecating moments is an asset, not something to be ashamed of when things go astray. In short, humility creates trust.

When UC Berkeley researchers studied these social tendencies, the results showed that people want to associate with someone who is comfortable being embarrassed in front of others. For example, the researchers videotaped 60 college students recounting embarrassing moments. The stories included typical sources of embarrassment, such as public flatulence, mistaking an overweight woman for being pregnant, or making other incorrect assumptions based on appearances. The team of researchers then rated the levels of embarrassment each subject showed.

When others saw these displays of public embarrassment, they were more cooperative and generous when they subsequently played games with the people who had been embarrassed. These studies suggest that there is no need to worry about awkward moments. In fact, a genuine response to such situations may even engender trust and friendships in the future.

I used to be quite hesitant about exposing my own insecurities and vulnerabilities, especially in a professional context. But I have learned that making fun of myself is often the safest thing to do, given the risk of offending others in unfamiliar situations. Talking about my fears, flaws, and follies often leads to an exchange of entertaining stories. Sometimes it leads to lasting connections. Being open about who I am — good, bad, and awkward — also saves me a lot of time because I am never pretending to be someone I'm not.

Connect for Speed and Creativity

It is easy to dismiss the need for close relationships at work until you focus on the bigger picture. Sure, you can get more done tomorrow if you put your head down and plow through a bunch of work. But if you fail to cultivate and maintain relationships, it will slow you down over time.

Anything of substance in life is created by working with others. I have yet to do anything very useful in isolation. Relationships boost achievement and create efficiency. If I need to explain something to a colleague I do not work with often, it may take 15 minutes. If I need to explain the same topic to a close friend at work, I can accomplish it in 60 seconds.

Friendships speed things up because emotions spread faster than words. When you see a friend at work, even if you don't say anything, you exchange an emotional state simply based on observing each other's facial expressions and body language. The closer you are with someone, the more likely you are to mirror each other's words and mannerisms. This serves a valuable purpose in helping you exchange even more information in less time.

Psychologist James Pennebaker has spent his career studying this topic. He said, "When two people start a conversation, they usually begin talking alike within a matter of seconds." When Pennebaker and his team looked at the synchronization of words married couples use, they found that word usage was similar during good points of marriages and less similar at low points. This suggests that the mirroring of another person's words may be a harbinger of a thriving relationship. But mirroring another person's body language, facial expressions, or words need not be reserved for your closest friendships; simply emulating the facial expressions or posture of a complete stranger can improve the quality of a conversation.

Friendships at work also come with a level of trust that allows for energizing and efficient interactions throughout the day. This is particularly relevant when a group is trying to solve a problem that requires creative thinking or when making a new product. When you get together with a group of people you enjoy spending time with, it puts you in a better mood. Experiments show that if you are in a better mood, your creativity increases and your thinking becomes more expansive. This helps explain why Gallup's research has shown that people who have "best friend"-caliber relationships at work are *seven times* as likely to be engaged in their job.

When researchers asked employees *how* they formed a close workplace friendship, they found that it takes about a year for an acquaintance at work to become a friend. The telltale sign of a friendship between co-workers was the amount of time they spent talking about topics unrelated to work. Then the next phase, a very close friendship at work, was marked by something less intuitive: sharing problems from one another's personal and work lives.

This self-disclosure was the central element of the strongest relationships.

Building great relationships at work takes time and effort. But it can start with something as simple as asking a colleague about his weekend or regularly going to lunch with one of your friends. The effort is worth it because the relationships you build are good for your work and well-being.

12

Take a Break *for* Relationships

When Bank of America first set up its call centers, it deliberately designed them for maximum efficiency in handling customer calls. Employees' breaks were timed so they didn't coincide with any of their peers' breaks. The intent was to ensure that the phone lines were always covered. Yet employee turnover was unacceptably high.

When the bank's leaders looked into the retention issue, they discovered that a lack of relationships and daily communication between employees was the root of the problem. This lack of cohesion was six times more predictive of performance than any other metric. Because of these findings, the bank's leaders changed the shift schedules to ensure that groups of employees could have lunch and take breaks at the same time.

Three months later, the same group of employees was handling calls 23 percent faster, and group cohesion had gone up by 18 percent. These increases translated into $15 million in added revenue for the company. The bank discovered that when employees had the opportunity to connect throughout the day, relationships inevitably formed and grew. And those relationships resulted in positive business outcomes for the bank.

Want What You Already Have

If you spend time with people who care about your development, you will grow. In turn, if you surround yourself with people who are hostile and negative, they will inevitably bring you down. The direct influence of people you spend time with affects everything from your well-being to your habits and choices.

For instance, when a friend smokes, it increases the odds that you'll smoke by 61 percent. Even if a friend of a friend (a second-degree connection) smokes, you are 29 percent more likely to smoke. This influence goes out to someone *three degrees* away from you in a network. If a friend of a friend of a friend smokes, you are 11 percent more likely to smoke. This is what researchers have dubbed the "contagion effect" in relationships, and it applies to everything from smoking to obesity levels.

Fortunately, the contagion effect in relationships works in a positive direction as well. If you have a friend who is happy, it increases your happiness levels even more than a

$10,000 increase in annual pay. When you do something kind for another person, he or she is more likely to pay it forward, as is the next person, and so on. Almost any investment in another person has an exponential return beyond what you can see in the moment.

Recent experiments suggest that the best way to produce sustainable increases in well-being is to appreciate what you already have and to continue creating new positive experiences with the people who matter most. When you value what you already have, not only will you grow, you won't feel the angst of wanting more. Any time you create experiences in the context of your existing resources and relationships, it has a compounding effect on your well-being.

Use Your Phone When You're Alone

Paying attention requires a little effort, but the rewards are great. Nothing adds more value to life than close social relationships. This is why it is so important to focus on the people you are with when you are with them.

There are countless distractions around you. In some cases, these distractions can be helpful. When I'm stuck in a long line at a grocery store, my digital pacifier (smartphone) is remarkably useful. Having the Internet in my pocket turns boring and frustrating moments into an opportunity to learn something or text a friend. However, these distractions create problems when you use them *while* spending time with friends, colleagues, or loved ones.

In fact, a 2014 study titled "The iPhone Effect" shows how the mere presence of a smartphone can ruin a conversation. In an experiment with 200 participants, researchers found that simply placing a mobile communication device on the table or having participants hold it in their hand was a detriment to their conversations. Any time the phone was visible, the quality of the conversation was rated as less fulfilling when compared with conversations that took place in the absence of mobile devices. People reported having higher levels of empathetic concern when phones were not visible.

Another study found that a visible cellphone decreased both attention and the ability to perform complex tasks. As I read more on this topic, I made some practical changes in my routine. I am much more conscious about the implicit message when I set my phone on a table, even if I do so just for convenience or comfort. It doesn't matter if my ringer is muted or my phone is off. Simply *seeing* a smartphone is bad for my concentration, others in the room, and the quality of my relationships.

Giving your undivided attention to others tells them how much you value their thoughts, opinions, and time. Intently listening to what another person is saying is a great way to forge new relationships and invest in your existing friendships. Dedicating a little time to understanding another person's perspective should also help you learn, grow, and expand your thinking.

Unfortunately, most of the time people are talking to you, you are not truly listening. You may *think* you are good at faking listening, but chances are, you're not. People read facial expressions in a matter of milliseconds. So when you're not paying full attention, other people can tell subconsciously, even if they don't say anything about it.

You have probably experienced how frustrating it can be when you're talking and it's obvious the other person has drifted off. According to one estimate, people listen at about 25 percent efficiency compared with what is possible, mostly because they can think much faster than they can listen, and that allows them to multitask.

Simply being in the same room with someone and making eye contact is not sufficient. Even if you aren't checking your smartphone messages while someone is talking, it's just as easy to tune out mentally. At times, I'm guilty of allowing my mind to wander on to what I plan to say next instead of listening to the other person's complete thoughts. Another challenge is that the average person listens for just 17 seconds before interrupting.

When you choose to have dedicated time with another person, such as dining, driving somewhere, or going on a walk, give that person your undivided attention. Talking on your phone, using apps, or reading a message tells others you don't value their time as much as you could. You chose to be with them, so make it count.

13

Put Experiences First

Think back on some of the most memorable vacations, trips, events, and experiences you have had throughout your life. As you reflect on these moments, you may notice how much joy you derive (even years later) from recalling the times you spent with people you care about. The best experiences create memories and well-being that last for years to come.

There is no better use of your financial resources than to spend them on meaningful experiences with other people. This may be the single most important discovery about how to use money effectively. Consider what occurs before, during, and after a trip with loved ones. If you plan a vacation well in advance, you experience several exciting months of anticipation. Then you have the actual experience of a trip with friends or family, followed by many years of fond memories.

Compare all of this goodwill with the cheap thrill of buying a new shirt for yourself, or even a new car. You might get a small spike in happiness immediately after the purchase, but the excitement of buying that new car fades quickly when you're sitting in traffic the following Monday morning. Even brief interpersonal experiences, such as going out to dinner with your spouse, a concert, or taking your kids to a sporting event, are a much better use of your financial resources.

One notable exception is spending on material goods that help you learn and grow, such as books, videos, sporting goods, and musical instruments. A 2014 study found that experience-oriented products *do* lead to increases in happiness.

According to San Francisco State University's Ryan Howell, a leading researcher on spending habits, people underestimate the extended value of experiential purchases. "What we find is that there's this huge misforecast," he said. "People think that experiences are only going to provide temporary happiness, but they actually provide both more happiness and more lasting value."

In Howell's studies, people's estimates of how happy they will be two weeks after a material purchase are pretty accurate. However, two weeks after an experiential purchase, people's ratings of whether their money was well spent are *106 percent higher* than their initial forecast. As Howell described, "Over time, material items are just crashing and life experiences are staying stable."

Even waiting in line is more enjoyable if it's for an experience — for instance, if you're waiting to buy tickets to a sporting event or concert. In addition to lasting longer than material purchases, experiential purchases can boost the well-being of multiple people at the same time. Every dollar you spend on an experience with another person is a well-being multiplier.

Yet most people, in the United States in particular, spend far too much on material goods relative to experiential purchases. In a typical American family, a whopping 50 percent of all annual expenditures are spent on cars and housing. This simply does not leave enough — at least on a percentage basis — for better investments, such as food, entertainment, trips, and other forms of recreation. In other developed economies, people spend just 30 to 40 percent of their resources on housing and transportation, which leaves two to three times as much discretionary income for experiential purchases.

One caveat is that spending on experiences won't work if you are doing it merely to impress other people. Howell noted, "Why you buy is just as important as what you buy . . . [W]hen people buy life experiences to impress others, it wipes out the well-being they receive from the purchase."

Howell's research reveals that experiences make people happier because they fill basic psychological needs for human growth, such as the need to feel competent, autonomous, and connected to others. Howell surveyed 241 people and discovered that their *motivation* for purchasing an experience determined whether their psychological needs would be met. He found that people who chose to buy life experiences — because those experiences were in line with their desires, interests, and values — were far more fulfilled as a result.

Buy Happiness (for Someone Else)

Michael Norton, a professor at Harvard Business School, has spent much of his career studying the relationship between finances and overall well-being. He has found that the raw accumulation of wealth is not what matters most. Norton explained, "It's not that it's bad to accumulate money; it's that people are focusing on something that doesn't pay off all that much."

What's more important is *how people spend* their money. One of the most common traps Norton has studied is when people think they can buy their way out of a rut in life by spending on themselves. In extreme cases, people can live in enormous houses and drive expensive cars but have no friends and be clinically depressed.

Fortunately, Norton's research also identifies the right ways to spend. Consider this example: If you go out right now and buy a coffee for yourself, it does little for your own well-being. But if you buy a coffee for someone else, it boosts your well-being and the other person's happiness at the same time. Norton's impression after conducting this research is that people leave a huge amount of happiness on the table by spending primarily on themselves. If you want to maximize both your money and your overall happiness at the same time, start thinking about how you can spend on other people.

When you are considering purchasing a material item, ask yourself how it will benefit another person or your relationships. If you can clearly see how the money you are about to spend will increase the well-being of people around you, it is a sound investment. However, if a purchase will give you a quick thrill right away but won't have any lasting impact for you or for others, skip it. Your relationships will be stronger as you put less emphasis and value on material possessions.

Plan Ahead for Well-Being

When you're planning an event, think about how it will increase the well-being of other people — before the actual experience. In 2006, while planning my honeymoon, I stumbled upon some of the earliest research examining the "anticipated utility" of experiences. The researchers measured and classified the degree to which anticipation, an event itself, and the memory of the event made distinct contributions to well-being.

It turned out that looking forward to a vacation or event provided even more happiness than the event itself. Even the memory contributed more to long-term well-being than the actual experience. While this surprised me at first, if you think back on any recent vacation, your memories may have more value than the experience of packing, going through airport security, sitting in the car for a long time, and so on.

After studying this research, I realized what a bad idea it was to keep my honeymoon travel plans as a surprise for my wife. So I went ahead and shared all the specifics about what we would be doing and where we were going. It did not take long to see how quickly this paid off. A few days later, I noticed that my wife was exploring the destination on her laptop and discussing it with a friend.

The next time you are planning an experience for other people, share as much detail as possible. If you are planning a weekend outing to a local park, tell your friends or your children the day before. Every time I have tried this with my two young kids, I find that the anticipation helps and enhances the experience itself.

For trips and events, try to plan several months in advance. A large study on this topic found that the effect of anticipating a vacation can increase well-being for weeks and even months. Even when an experience does not go exactly as you had hoped or planned, it is likely to get better with age. Unlike material goods, which you adapt to and forget about over time, people tend to recall shared experiences with rose-colored glasses. So if it rains while you are at the beach or the amusement park is overcrowded, don't despair. It will be a fond memory of family bonding down the road.

14

Avoid Flying Solo

The best moments in life rarely happen while you are sitting around alone. The times that make life worthwhile occur in the company of your closest relationships. However, there is too much time and effort focused on individual achievement. From schooling to work to personal goals, people spend a disproportionate amount of time working on solitary pursuits.

When researchers ask people to reconstruct the most positive and negative experiences of their lives, they consistently describe social events as their most influential memories over a lifetime. Across a series of four studies, participants recalled the moments when close relationships began or ended, when they fell in love, or when the loss of another person broke their heart. One of the study's co-authors summarized, "In short, it was the moments of connecting to others that touched people's lives the most."

Participants consistently rated events with other people as more influential than solitary experiences. Independent events or individual achievements, such as winning awards or completing tasks, did not affect participants the most. Instead, the researchers concluded, social experiences "gain their emotional punch from our need to belong."

Think about a few of your own priorities. Whether it's finishing a big project at work, getting a degree, or running a half marathon, consider whether your goal involves another person or is a solitary effort. There is nothing wrong with working on important individual milestones as long as you understand that they may not be the memories you treasure 25 years from now.

Win While Others Succeed

The fundamental premise of a relationship is that two people are better off together than they are divided. You should experience more enjoyment when you are with your spouse than when you are apart. A friendship at work should produce more mutual enjoyment or achievement than if you were working independently. However, it is easy to take this for granted.

A team of researchers that studied new social connections as part of an experiment found that simple conversations made a big difference. When strangers were instructed to get to know one another for 10 minutes, it boosted their subsequent performance on a variety of common tasks. But if these conversations had a competitive edge, the benefit and improvement disappeared.

This experiment may help explain why it is so important to assume positive intent every time you meet another person. When both parties assume positive intent, there is a better chance they will achieve their shared goals and perhaps be a little happier in the process. However, if either person entering into an encounter views it as a competition, the interaction may be doomed from the start.

There is an entire body of literature on what political scientists call "zero-sum" situations. Zero-sum means two parties walk into a scenario in which each person is fighting to win a fixed portion of a limited pie. So if I get 60 percent, the best you can do is get 40 percent. In athletics and politics, there are certainly times when a short-term sum is fixed. Yet viewing a relationship as a zero-sum game is the fastest way to set it up for failure.

You win; someone else loses. The zero-sum mentality is engrained at a young age. Especially in competitive cultures and societies, there is an even more distinct win-versus-loss perspective. An athlete or team wins the gold medal, World Cup, or Super Bowl. The team that comes in second is the loser.

When it comes to the work you do, in many cases, *others win more when you succeed.* If you build a successful product or business, you create jobs, suppliers, and customers. You also add to the overall economy. Almost anything you do in your work creates more value than you are likely to extract from competitors or rivals. As a result, work teams and organizations that focus the most attention on catching up or beating the competition are the least likely to succeed.

Use Pro-Social Incentives

When you think about incentives, individual rewards for achievement usually come to mind. Yet personal rewards are often ineffective, perhaps because they rely on the assumption that people are concerned primarily with their own self-interest — or at least more than they are with helping other people.

However, a great deal of research suggests that the desire to help other people is part of what makes you human. Scientists are exploring whether giving can be a much more powerful motivator than receiving. A fascinating series of three experiments led by Duke's Lalin Anik indicates that pro-social incentives help people achieve more and be more satisfied while doing so.

In one of the experiments, good work was rewarded with money that participants were directed to spend on a bill, expense, or gift for themselves. In contrast, participants in the "pro-social group" were given an incentive but instructed to spend the money on a teammate instead. Even though the study was conducted with a group of pharmaceutical salespeople (which is a traditionally competitive profession), the team that had incentive to do good *for someone else* saw greater gains in performance than the team with a more selfish incentive.

A second study was conducted with sports teams, using the same design of asking players to spend money on themselves or their teammates. The teams assigned to the pro-social condition had a dramatic improvement in their winning percentage. The third experiment Anik and team conducted gave bankers a $50 bonus, which they were instructed to donate to a charity on behalf of their company. When compared with a control group, the group assigned the pro-social donation saw significant gains in happiness and job satisfaction.

When you want to motivate people to do great work, give them an incentive that will serve another person or benefit the entire team. When your friends, colleagues, spouse, or children accomplish something, try giving them a gift that keeps giving. Structure donations of time or resources. Plan an outing that includes some of their closest friends. If it is a material gift, make it one they can share with a group of people, like a gift certificate to a restaurant. Try this when motivating yourself and others, and see if you can set a cycle in motion. Remember that everyone is wired to get more of a boost from giving than from receiving.

15

Build a Cumulative Advantage

When you focus on other people's shortcomings, they lose confidence in their abilities. But if you focus on their hard work and successes, you produce a sustainable increase in their self-confidence. What's more, researchers have discovered that the earlier in life you focus on a person's daily successes, the greater the gains over time.

Scientists reviewed studies that followed more than 7,000 people for 25 years. They found that confidence at a young age led to what they described as a "cumulative advantage" — the careers of confident individuals took off at an exponential pace compared with those who had lower levels of self-confidence. The benefits continued to increase by the year. The earlier people gained self-confidence, the more measurable the difference, even in their physical health. The members of the group with higher self-confidence at a young age started at about the same baseline level of health, but they had just one-third as many health problems 25 years later.

Help the people around you understand what gives them a natural charge. Think about your social circles, and identify someone who may need a little encouragement. Helping others see their daily successes more clearly can lead to rapid growth. Every person has hidden talent waiting to be uncovered. In some cases, you may be the only person who has spotted that unique strength — so be sure to call it out when you see it. As I learned from personal experience, a few encouraging words can go a long way.

Help Someone See What Could Be

As a result of my grandfather, Don Clifton's, lifelong study of strengths, I was raised in an environment in which my family was looking for early traces of talent at every turn. By the time I was five, they had spotted my deep interest in reading. When I was nine, my grandfather noticed some entrepreneurial talent and helped me start a little business selling snacks. He helped me find space and figure out how to buy snacks in bulk. And he taught me some basic financial concepts. But the most valuable lessons I learned were about people, interactions, and relationships.

Throughout my grade school, high school, and college years, it became clear to me that my talents and interests were in the areas of business, research, and anything involving technology. When I graduated from college in 1998, Don asked me if I would work with him to bring his research on strengths to a wider audience through technology and this new thing called the Internet. I spent the next few years working with Don and our team to create an online strength-based assessment, dubbed StrengthsFinder. But in the midst of all the excitement around this new project, Don found out he had Stage IV gastroesophageal cancer and most likely only a few months left to live.

Given that I had been battling cancer for a decade at the time, I used my knowledge and dedicated all my time to helping my grandfather extend his life as much as possible. Don and I assembled all the research we could find on the topic as we traveled to different medical centers for treatment. In the midst of this ordeal, I remembered that Don had once told me he thought it was crazy that people wait until someone is gone to say kind things in a eulogy.

So I stayed up late for several nights and wrote a very long and emotional letter to my grandfather, explaining how much he had influenced my life over the years. It was essentially a eulogy written to someone who was still alive. This letter told my personal story about battling cancer as a teenager and went into great depth about what a difference my grandfather's ideas and approach to life made during this time. I explained how his love, caring, and thinking essentially built a reserve that helped me make it through all of my health challenges in relatively good shape.

Because I had almost no confidence in my ability to communicate effectively in writing, I was hesitant to even share this heartfelt letter with Don—but given the circumstances, I decided to give it to him. When he read it, he was deeply moved and grateful. That part did not surprise me, but a brief interaction we had a few days later caught me off guard.

Don told me that after reading the letter multiple times, he thought I had a real talent for bringing things to life with words. This was something *no one* had ever suggested, let alone stated explicitly. He asked if I would be willing to share my personal story from the letter in a book. As long as somebody else was doing the writing, I figured that would be okay.

Then Don asked me if I would help him *write* that book over the next *two months*. This was the only time he ever acknowledged the reality of his condition in our conversations. So I agreed to give it a shot and do my best, knowing that my grandfather had quite a bit of wisdom that could benefit other people. We worked tirelessly over the next couple of months and were able to finish our first draft of the book, *How Full Is Your Bucket?*, just before Don passed away. That book has since helped my grandfather's work reach millions of people, and we even turned it into a children's book that is now used in classrooms around the world.

Develop the Ultimate Strength

This personal experience showed me how a single interaction and observation can have a lifelong influence. After nearly three decades of exploring my own talent, having great people around me, and taking countless strengths assessments, writing was the last thing I ever planned to do. Then one person said he spotted a talent worthy of investment, and that insight continues to influence how I now spend my time every day. The more I reflect on this experience, the more I realize that the ultimate strength is finding and developing talent in others.

One of the best ways to help another person grow is through the right types of praise and recognition. Simply telling someone they did a "good job" on a project is nice but not very helpful, especially if your comments lack sincerity. In fact, insincere positive remarks could be even more toxic and detrimental than negative comments.

In addition to being sincere, words that give people a positive charge should be as specific as possible. A series of six experiments published in 2014 reveals why specificity is essential for motivating other people. Participants in one experiment were asked to "give those who need bone marrow transplants greater hope." Phrasing the goal that way was less motivating compared with a request for participants to "give those who need bone marrow transplants a better chance of finding a donor." It was also more effective when researchers asked participants to "increase recycling" rather than "save the environment."

The more specific your language is during even brief interactions, the greater the influence. As you help other people see what they do best, you will help them build a cumulative advantage over time. You could also make a contribution to their future health and well-being that you may not be able to see in the moment.

11%
of people had a great deal
of energy yesterday

16

Put Your Own Health First

Some of the most caring people also tend to be the least healthy. This is what I observed, time and time again, while spending the last few years focused on health and well-being. After writing the book *Eat Move Sleep*, which I will draw from throughout the next three chapters, I heard from thousands of people who were struggling with their personal health and a general lack of energy.

Surprisingly, workers in the professions I admire most, such as nursing, are often the least healthy. One study found that 55 percent of nurses are overweight or obese. If there is any group that needs to be healthier and set a good example, it is people working in healthcare. As I listened to the stories of workers across professions, from educators to business leaders, it was clear that some of the most mission-driven people have spent a lifetime putting everyone else's needs before their own.

While this is admirable on many levels and consistent with the focus of this book, it is a costly mistake. Even if you are determined to be the least selfish person on the planet and do nothing but serve other people, you need the daily energy to do so effectively. When I spoke with hospice nurses who were always putting the needs of terminally ill patients and their families first, the last thing they were thinking about was their own health and energy. Yet when I asked them what it took to be their very best at helping people during this time of need, they acknowledged that they could be of far more service if they invested time in their own health and energy.

A study of more than 30,000 nurses across Europe found that those who work long shifts (more than 12 hours) are 32 percent more likely to rate the quality of care on their ward as poor, compared with nurses working eight-hour shifts. They were also 41 percent more likely to report failing or poor standards of safety on their ward. In many cases, working longer hours is a *disservice* to those you intend to serve.

I have seen this phenomenon in businesses all around the world. There is often an implicit pressure, for leaders in particular, to be the first ones in to the office, to work the longest days, and to claim they need very little sleep. Yet the last thing businesses need is star performers in the workplace burning out because they have a routine that is unsustainable. The research my team conducted on this topic found that people who have very high energy levels in a given day are more than *three times* as likely to be completely engaged in their work that same day.

If you want to make a difference — not just today, but for many years to come — you need to *put your health and energy ahead of all else*. If you are wiped out from working around the clock, subsisting on food from a vending machine, and not making time for daily exercise, then there is no way you'll be effective at helping your friends, family, colleagues, patients, or customers. The good news is that making choices to improve your energy does not require a complex grand plan. It all starts with the next choice you make.

Use Short-Term Thinking for Better Health

As I mentioned at the beginning of the book, I have spent the last 20-plus years battling various cancers and trying to improve my odds of living longer. An important lesson from my own experience is that even a profound threat to one's mortality is a poor motivator for making better decisions today. Knowing that it may help prevent cancer several years down the road does not motivate me to exercise on a daily basis. Most people don't stop before eating a fast-food meal to contemplate how doing so regularly could increase their long-term risk of heart disease.

All of the knowledge about creating healthier lifestyles does very little good until it leads to a change in daily behavior. This is why I've spent a great deal of time over the last decade organizing the most practical ideas for better health and more energy. As I read through a wide range of research, I look for studies that connect better daily decisions with short-term wins and incentives. While I'm not a physician or an expert on these topics, I use my background as a patient and researcher to find the most pragmatic ideas for healthier choices.

Making the connection between better decisions and my daily energy levels has done far more to change my behavior than all I have learned about longer term health consequences. When I have an important day ahead, I make sure to get some activity in the morning so I'm in a better mood and my thinking is sharper. I base my decisions about what to eat for lunch on whether the meal will help sustain my energy into the afternoon and evening. If I am active throughout the day and eat well, I know that I will then have a better night's sleep, which will give me a head start on the next day.

It is remarkable how quickly these small choices accumulate, for better and for worse. A breakfast filled with sweet, baked, or fried foods makes it almost impossible to get back on track for the rest of the day. On days when I have to sit on an airplane or in a meeting for several hours, I am physically and mentally wiped out from inactivity. A single night of poor sleep usually makes me grumpy and impairs my ability to work effectively.

When things go wrong in any one of these three areas — eating, moving, or sleeping — it throws everything else off course. A poor night of sleep leads to skipping a workout, lousy food choices, and so on. The good news is, doing just one of these things well can lead to an upward spiral in the other two areas. Contrary to my original expectations, experimental research suggests that it is a good idea to tackle multiple elements of health at the same time.

Think about how your eating, moving, and sleeping influence each other every day. Doing all three well is the key to having more energy throughout the day. When you need to be your very best — for work, family, and friends — start by ensuring that you have adequate energy to be fully charged.

17

Eat Your Way to a Better Day

The foods you eat directly influence your energy levels throughout the day, yet it is often difficult to know what foods to eat and which ones to avoid. Many people, myself included, have gravitated toward blunt measures of overall consumption, like total calorie count. Unfortunately, calories are not a measure of food quality.

A landmark Harvard University study that tracked more than 100,000 people over two decades makes it clear that the quality of what you eat is more important than quantity alone. This study revealed that the types of food you consume influence your health more than your total caloric intake. Consuming 300 calories' worth of spinach is not the same as eating a sugar cookie with 300 calories. Yet most people I speak with continue to believe the age-old myth of "everything in moderation." As the study's lead author Dariush Mozaffarian put it, the moderation myth is really "just an excuse to eat whatever we want."

Eating well is much easier when you begin with the right foods. Instead of jumping from one fad diet to the next, you can build the core elements of eating healthy into something much more sustainable.

Start with the basics: Avoid fried foods. Eat fewer refined carbohydrates. Eliminate as much added sugar as possible. Build meals around vegetables. Substitute whole fruit for sweets. Drink more water, tea, and coffee instead of soda or other sweetened drinks.

There is a lot of conflicting advice today about what is good and what is bad in terms of diet. But no one is making the case that you should eat more donuts and fewer apples. Eating right does not need to be overly complicated.

Building your routine around the right foods is not only sustainable, it's enjoyable. Start by eating more foods that are a good source of daily energy. This is a lot easier than jumping on the latest diet bandwagon or going to extremes.

It is important to note that consuming the right foods for your health and energy is very different from schemes to lose 10 pounds in 30 days. The human body takes quite a bit of time to react to dietary changes — in many cases, a year or more. Make better daily choices with the idea of boosting your energy so you do not grow impatient waiting for drastic physical changes, which typically take more time.

Make Every Bite Count

Every time you take a bite of food, you are making a small yet important choice. Each drink requires yet another small decision. When you make a choice that does more good than harm, such as opting for a salad over a burger, the resulting net gain gives your body a positive charge. Deciding to drink a sugary soda instead of water produces a net loss.

Most meals contain both good and bad ingredients, such as high nutrient content but an excess of sugar. You probably eat some foods that are less than ideal several times a day. But try to do some mental accounting. Based on all you know about the components of a certain item or meal, ask yourself if what you are about to eat is a net gain or loss. As you continue to ask this question, you should become better at making decisions in the moment.

Most people eat more refined (processed) carbohydrates than they need relative to the amount of protein they consume. Yet large-scale studies on this topic show that even modest increases in protein intake, when coupled with a reduction in carbohydrates, improve health. One way to dig beneath the headline of total calories on a menu or box is to look at the ratio of carbohydrates to proteins.

I started doing this a few years ago, and it is a good shortcut when scanning packaged items in a grocery store or basic nutritional information on a menu. The mixed nuts I carry with me in my bag as a standby snack or the palak paneer (an Indian dish of spinach and cheese) that

I eat for lunch are nearly a one-to-one ratio of carbs to proteins. At a minimum, I try to avoid foods that have higher than a 5-to-1 carbs to proteins ratio. For reference, most snack chips or cereals have a 10-to-1 ratio.

A 2014 study from the University of Missouri found that consuming protein in the morning increases levels of dopamine, a brain chemical involved in moderating impulses, which reduces subsequent cravings for both sweet and savory foods. But if you skip breakfast, it causes your body to store additional fat and increases your waistline over time. To stay sharp and slim, it's critical to eat the right foods early in the day.

Sugar-filled cereals and breakfast bars may give you a quick energy boost, but the effect will not last. In contrast, eating foods with a low glycemic index in the morning prevents spikes in blood sugar later in the day, which could make for better choices in the afternoon and evening. Instead of traditional cereals for breakfast, consider foods like egg whites, berries, lean meats, salmon, nuts, seeds, vegetable-based shakes, or other options that are not filled with added sugars.

Maintaining a better balance of carbohydrates to proteins throughout the day should boost your energy and improve your health over time. The other thing to look for — on any bag, box, or menu — is total grams of sugar. When it comes to this metric, the closer to zero, the better. There is absolutely no dietary need for any added sugar — a toxin that fuels diabetes, obesity, heart disease, and cancer.

Sugar substitutes are not much better; they simply lead you to crave more sweet foods.

Set Better Defaults

Dietary habits usually follow the path of least resistance. While this tendency sounds like a flaw, it can also be advantageous. If you make a list of healthy foods before you go grocery shopping, you are less likely to stock up on impulse choices. And you've probably heard that it is better to shop for food when your stomach is full instead of when you are hungry.

When I visit my neighborhood grocery store, I spend the majority of my time in the fresh produce and seafood sections. I know that if I can avoid the middle aisles that are loaded with unhealthy and processed items, those things will not wind up in my cart. By now, I have learned that anything that goes in my cart makes it home, and whatever makes it home ends up in my stomach.

You are also far more likely to eat what you can see in plain view. Organize the foods in your kitchen and pantry so the best choices are most visible and easily accessible. It also helps to hide poor choices in inconvenient places. An even better idea is to clean out your pantry and cabinets and simply get rid of anything with low nutritional value that you may be tempted to eat.

Put fruits, vegetables, and other healthy options at eye level in your refrigerator, or leave them out on the counter or table. Even when you aren't hungry, simply seeing these items will plant a seed in your mind for your next snack. Also consider taking small bags of nuts, fruits, or vegetables with you when you are away from home. That way, you can satisfy a mid-afternoon craving even if no good options are available. The more you plan to make healthy choices *in advance*, the less willpower you will need to avoid tempting last-minute decisions.

Find Food That Charges Your Mood

Standing on the bathroom scale at age 38, Jeremy Wright was shocked by what he saw. The scale topped 225. So he went to see his physician and received even more sobering news: his fasting blood sugar was 134, putting him on the precipice of diabetes.

After stepping on his scale that day, Wright began making small changes to his lifestyle that have added up in the year since. Now, before making any decision, he asks himself if he's helping or hurting his health. He goes to the gym five days a week, even if it means leaving work an hour earlier. When he works from home, he stands. He's cut down on the carbs and sweets. When he snacks during the day, it's on nuts and water.

Wright said he started feeling better almost immediately after making these changes. Today, his weight has dropped from over 225 to 190. His waist size has gone from 40 to 34. His shirts have gone from extra large to large. His blood sugar is normal. And most important, he has more energy. Even though he's working fewer hours, he gets more done.

The food you eat every day not only influences your energy levels, it also clearly affects your mood. When researchers study the relationship between what people eat and mental health, it is clear that some foods give you a positive charge, while other foods have the opposite effect. Eating too much fatty food, for example, can make you lethargic and moody. A 2014 study suggests that highly processed foods with added sugar may also contribute to laziness.

One experiment on this topic found that people who consumed more trans-fatty acids were more aggressive and irritable as a result. These findings were so pronounced, one of the researchers suggested that places like schools and prisons should reconsider serving unhealthy foods because they might be dangerous for others in these environments. Even "comfort foods" like baked goods actually have the opposite effect of comfort and are likely to make people more depressed.

Making better dietary choices, on the other hand, can improve your daily health and well-being. Studies suggest that on days when you eat more fruits and vegetables, you feel calmer and happier and have more energy than normal. Every time you decide what to eat, you shape your days and your interactions with others.

18

Learn to Walk Before You Run

Being active *throughout the day* is the key to staying energized. Even 30–60 minutes of exercise a day will not cut it if you spend the rest of your day sitting around. Moving around and getting more activity every hour is what will keep you fully charged.

People now spend more time sitting down (9.3 hours) than sleeping in a day. But the human body is not built for a sedentary lifestyle, which creates a host of problems. Even watching your diet and exercising every day is not enough to offset several hours of sitting. A 2014 study estimates that every two hours of sitting cancels out the benefits of 20 minutes of exercise.

When researchers from the National Institutes of Health followed more than 200,000 people for a decade, they found that even seven hours of moderate to vigorous physical activity a week was not enough to protect against the hazards of excessive sitting. Even the most active group they studied — people who exercised more than seven hours every week — had a 50 percent greater risk of death and doubled their odds of dying from heart disease if they were also in the group that sat the most throughout the day.

Keep Sitting From Sapping Your Energy

Sitting may be the most underrated health threat of this generation. It subtly erodes people's health over time. On a global level, inactivity now kills more people than cigarettes do. A recent study from the Mayo Clinic found that the average American spends more than 15 hours per day sleeping and sitting. Obese men and women spend less than one minute per day engaged in vigorous activity.

Consider how the time you spend sitting down accumulates over the span of a single day. Maybe you sit down for a while to watch the morning news and eat breakfast. Then you have a commute that adds another hour of sitting. After arriving at work, you spend 8 or 10 hours in an office chair. After your commute back home, you have a nice sit-down dinner with family and then watch an hour or two of television before going to bed.

While this is a normal day for some people, I'm hoping you have a bit more activity in your daily routine. When you look at a typical day, you can most likely identify long periods of time when you are seated. What's not as easy to see is the way this "sitting disease" takes a physical toll.

When you sit down, the electrical activity in your leg muscles shuts off quickly. Your rate of burning calories drops to just one per minute. The enzymes that help break down fat fall by 90 percent. After sitting for two hours, your good cholesterol drops by 20 percent.

However, sitting for several hours a day is almost unavoidable for many people, so the challenge is to build as much movement into your day as possible. Little things like stretching and standing a couple of times every hour make a difference.

Walking increases energy levels by about 150 percent. Taking the stairs burns twice as many calories as walking. Instead of viewing a slightly longer walk as something you don't have time for, view it as an opportunity to add a little activity to your day.

Study your surroundings to determine how you can reduce completely sedentary time. The way life has become built around convenience means that many of the things you need are now within arm's reach. So you can sit for long periods without having to move around and interact with others. Try to turn this around by organizing your home and office to encourage movement more than convenience.

Small bursts of activity will do as much for your mind as they will for your physical energy. Regular breaks from mental tasks have been shown to increase both creativity and productivity. You simply think better when you move more. A deluge of research published over the last few years has shown how even brief periods of activity improve learning and attention and help your brain function more effectively.

Measure to Move More

One of the best ways to increase your activity levels is to measure how much you move every day. While this is a golden era for wearable health-tracking devices, you can also accomplish this goal with an inexpensive pedometer. As part of one experiment, when people were assigned to wear a pedometer, they walked an extra mile per day, compared with a control group. What's more, participants in this group saw their overall activity levels go up by 27 percent as a byproduct of measuring their movement.

When I first started tracking my daily activity in 2009 using a small clip-on device called a Fitbit, my typical day consisted of just 5,000 steps. Even though I considered myself fairly active at the time, I had no idea how sedentary my lifestyle had become. A year after I started tracking my movement, I was averaging 8,000 steps per day. Today, I have a rule for myself that I need to hit 10,000 steps before I go to sleep, even on days filled with travel in cars or on planes.

On my best days, when I'm using a homemade workstation I built atop an old treadmill, I get about 30,000 steps a day. While this may sound like a lot of activity to squeeze into a day, I usually get far more work done on these days because all that walking boosts my energy levels. Each night before I go to bed, the last thing I look at is my total step and distance count for the day. This number has become my single best gauge for whether I had a good day or a sluggish and stressful day.

Based on the research I've studied, 10,000 steps per day is a good target for overall activity. This equates to about five miles, which is not as intimidating as it sounds once you start to add up all your daily movement. At the other end of the spectrum, people who walk fewer than 5,500 steps a day are considered sedentary. Fortunately, going from the low end of this continuum to the recommended 10,000 steps can lead to significant health benefits in the short term as well as the long run.

Get a 12-Hour Charge in 20 Minutes

You may have noticed how being active can boost your daily well-being. An experiment on this topic suggests that the improvement in mood may be even more durable over time than I would have guessed. When researchers assigned one group of participants in a study to do 20 minutes of a moderate-intensity workout, they found that the participants had a much better mood immediately following the exercise than a control group who did not exercise. What surprised researchers was how long this increase in mood lasted. Those who exercised continued to feel better throughout the day. Even two, four, eight, and twelve hours later, they were in a better mood than the control group.

Working out in the evening is better than no activity at all, but if you work out late in the day, you essentially sleep through and miss the boost in mood that exercise produces. The more activity you get the morning, the less likely that 12-hour mood boost will go to waste. Activity early in the day could also help you burn more calories throughout the day.

Instead of thinking about exercise in the morning as something that will drain your energy, as it sometimes does over the first few days of a new routine, keep in mind that it will eventually give you more energy throughout the day. Even brief activity can produce major gains in creativity and productivity.

You simply think better when you are active. "Research shows that when we exercise, blood pressure and blood flow increase everywhere in the body, including the brain. More blood means more energy and oxygen, which makes our brain perform better," explained the University of Illinois's Justin Rhodes. What's more, activating these pathways in the brain and body does not require extraordinary effort.

Moving more throughout the day starts with simple changes. Walk and stand in meetings to keep focused and energized. Use a headset so you can move around while you're on the phone. If possible, finding a way to work on your computer while standing or walking is even better. The key is to start engineering a little activity into your routine today.

19

Sleep Longer to Achieve More

While growing up in a hardworking city in the Midwest, I learned that needing sleep was a sign of weakness. The adults I looked up to constantly boasted about running on limited sleep. I now understand that this stemmed from a good-natured work ethic, but it caused me to view sleep as the very first expense I should cut out of my day.

Over the last decade, however, I have learned that one less hour of sleep is not equal to an extra hour of achievement or enjoyment. Instead, the exact opposite occurs. When you miss an hour of sleep, it decreases your well-being, productivity, health, and ability to think. Yet sleep continues to be the first thing people sacrifice. I fell into this trap for many years, until I realized my assumptions about sacrificing sleep were in direct conflict with a great deal of research.

When I read K. Anders Ericsson's landmark studies of elite performance, I noticed that many people overlooked a factor that significantly influenced performance. While many concentrated on his findings relevant to 10,000 hours of deliberate practice, the other factor that differentiated top performance was sleep. The best performers in these studies slept for 8 hours and 36 minutes per night on average. The average American, in contrast, gets just 6 hours and 51 minutes of sleep on weeknights.

Ericsson's studies of elite performers — which included musicians, athletes, actors, and chess players — also suggest that resting more frequently boosts achievement. Much like the most effective workers I discussed earlier, elite performers in these professions also work in bursts. Ericsson found that they take frequent breaks to avoid exhaustion and to ensure that they fully recharge. This allows them to keep improving and perfecting their craft.

When you work on a task for too long, it degrades your performance. To avoid diminishing returns, work in bursts, take regular breaks, and make sure that you get enough sleep. The next time you need an extra hour of energy, try adding an hour of sleep.

Don't Show Up for Work After a Six-Pack

The less you sleep, the less you can achieve. A study from Harvard Medical School found that lack of sleep is costing the American economy $63 billion a year in lost productivity alone. One of the study's authors noted, "Americans are not missing work because of insomnia. They are still going to their jobs but they're accomplishing less because they're tired. In an information-based economy, it's difficult to find a condition that has a greater effect on productivity."

When you're working without sufficient sleep, you are a different person — and it shows. One study suggests that losing 90 minutes of sleep can reduce daytime alertness by nearly one-third. Amid all the things you need to do in a day, losing this much of your normal alertness creates a serious deficit.

To put this in perspective, think about it from someone else's standpoint. The person I want to fly my airplane, teach my children, or lead the company I work for tomorrow is the one who sleeps soundly tonight. Yet people in these essential roles are often the ones who think they need the least sleep. A full one-third of workers may be getting fewer than six hours of sleep on a typical night. In some cases, the consequences go far beyond lost productivity.

Sleepless driving can be just as dangerous as driving drunk. One scientist who studied this extensively claims that four hours of sleep loss produces as much impairment as a six-pack of beer. An entire night of sleep loss is equivalent to a blood alcohol level of 0.19 percent, which is double most legal limits for intoxication. There is a good reason why doctors and pilots now have mandated periods of rest before working. If you look at major transportation incidents involving cars, trains, and planes, sleeplessness is a common cause of accidental deaths.

Get a Vaccine for the Common Cold

Sleeping well may have even more practical value when it comes to preventing the common cold. As part of one study, participants agreed to be quarantined and given nasal drops containing rhinovirus (the common cold). Researchers had tracked these participants' sleep quality for fourteen nights prior to administering the rhinovirus. The subjects were then monitored for the next five days to see if they developed a cold.

The results showed that participants who averaged fewer than seven hours of sleep a night before being exposed to the rhinovirus were nearly *three times* as likely to catch a cold following exposure. This experiment also revealed that total time in bed was not the most important metric. As you have probably experienced, you can spend eight hours tossing and turning in bed and get just six hours of good sleep.

For that reason, the researchers also graded participants' sleep quality, or "sleep efficiency," and assigned a score to each person. This calculation factored in what time people went to sleep in relation to when they awoke, how much time they spent in bed before falling asleep, how many times they woke during the night, and how long they were up throughout the night. The sleep efficiency metric was an even more powerful predictor of which participants developed a cold.

Study participants who had lower sleep efficiency over the 14-day period before exposure to the rhinovirus were *5.5 times as likely to develop a cold*. This compares with the threefold increase based solely on duration of sleep. As with other areas of health, quality of sleep beats quantity by a wide margin. Even though you cannot see what's going on inside your body, it's clear that a sound night of sleep has a direct effect on your near-term physiological health.

Fight Light, Heat, and Noise

While getting seven to eight hours of sound sleep each night is easier said than done, there are adjustments you can make to improve your odds of a good night's sleep. And what you do in the hours before you go to bed could matter most.

More than 90 percent of Americans use electronic communications in the hour before they go to bed. Allowing such stressors into your pre-sleep time is only going to keep you awake. A 2014 study suggests that late-night smartphone use is bad for your work the following day. This research found that using a smartphone late at night not only leads to poor sleep but also creates fatigue and lower engagement in the workplace.

The light from electronic devices alone can suppress your melatonin levels by as much as 20 percent, which is a direct threat to sleep quality. To avoid that, impose a moratorium on all electronic devices in the hour before your normal bedtime. Be cautious about bright light from any sources in the hours leading up to your bedtime. While natural light in the middle of the day can lead to better sleep and is good for productivity, dimming lights throughout the evening can help you sleep better.

Creating the right environment in your bedroom can give you a head start on a good night's sleep. It is easier to sleep in a room that is a few degrees cooler than the temperature you are accustomed to throughout the day. The reduced temperature prevents your natural body clock from waking you up in the middle of the night.

The same principle applies to noise. If your sleep is often disrupted by random sounds, use a white-noise app or device to keep noises from waking you throughout the night. Creating a routine in which you eliminate as much variance as possible is critical for a good night of sleep.

Prioritize seven to eight hours of high-quality sleep ahead of all else. You will be more likely to have a good workout, get more done at your job, and treat your loved ones better when you put sleep first. Keep in mind that every hour of sleep does not cost you in terms of efficiency. Instead, it will give you a positive charge for the upcoming day.

20

Eat, Move, and Sleep
to De-Stress

Of all the ways that eating, moving, and sleeping well influence your health, how they can buffer against stress may be the most remarkable. Scientists have known for some time that stressors accumulate and contribute to aging at a cellular level. Telomeres, which are protective caps at the ends of your chromosomes that affect how quickly cells age, protect your cells from stressors. As these telomeres shorten and their structural integrity weakens, cells age and die.

Telomeres shorten as you age, and they have also been shown to decrease in length as a result of stress. A team of University of California, San Francisco researchers was surprised by the degree to which the shortening of telomeres can be slowed — even in the face of stressors. As part of a remarkable yearlong study, 239 women provided blood samples for telomere measurement and reported on stressful events that occurred throughout the year. Researchers also tracked their eating, moving, and sleeping patterns during the study.

The researchers found that women who were exposed to more stressors throughout the year saw significant reduction in telomere length. This in itself was notable, as it was the first study to show that stressors can create substantial changes in just one year. However, when researchers looked at the group of women who maintained healthy lifestyles — in how they ate, moved, and slept — the accumulation of life stressors did *not* lead to significant shortening of telomeres. As lead author Eli Puterman summarized, the results suggest that "keeping active and eating and sleeping well during periods of high stress are particularly important to attenuate the accelerated aging of our immune cells."

Keep Stress From Snowballing

When wet and heavy snow falls on my sidewalk, I know that I need to start shoveling well before the snowfall ends. If I wait too long, the snow will be too deep and heavy for me to shovel. There is also likely to be a layer of ice at the bottom that is almost impossible to crack through. Stress accumulates in a similar manner.

This is why you should keep stress from piling up in the first place. Of all the things in life that can derail a good day, stress is the most common culprit. While a little stress is not a problem and can sometimes even be helpful, chronic stress creates an extraordinary amount of damage over time. Excessive stress accelerates aging and increases the risk of heart disease, stroke, cancer, and early death. These negative effects are the product of days when stressors elevate cortisol levels and increase inflammation throughout the body.

For many years, I thought of stress as something that ruins a day now and then, and not much else. I figured that a few days or weeks of excessive stress were fine because I could simply "shut it off." Yet this is clearly not the case. Every day, week, and month of undue stress is cumulative. As stressful days compile, your energy levels, health, and relationships worsen. There is almost no way you can feel energized when you're dealing with chronic stressors.

Consider some of the things that regularly create stress in your life. Map out how you can avoid these situations in the first place, or at least minimize the daily stress they cause. Rarely, if ever, is putting up with intense stress worth the consequences for your health and well-being.

Avoid Secondhand Stress

Difficult interactions with other people are at the root of most people's stress. If your boss is under a great deal of pressure and pushing you to hit unrealistic deadlines, his stress becomes yours. When a spouse or close friend is stressed out, even about something unrelated to your relationship, you can inherit that stress in no time.

When you hear the word "stress," consider whom you automatically associate with that word. It is likely that one or more people in your social networks, from friends to family to colleagues, run at a slightly faster pace than others. This is natural. Some people are more laid-back in general and have an easygoing personality. Others live at a faster tempo and thrive on having a lot of things going on at once. And some people become easily upset or angry about things that others take in stride.

I happen to be one of those people who enjoys constant activity and moving quickly. A good day for me is getting a lot of things done in a condensed period of time and then unwinding with friends and family afterward. But I have realized that when I am in my fast-paced mode, other people mistake it for stress. As a result, they see me pushing through a day without much patience, and it makes them more stressed out. This is certainly not my intent, but I can see the unintended consequences of the tension I project.

If this sounds familiar, be a little more conscious of what your emotional temperature and words do to other people. When you have a lot going on, how do you come across to your colleagues, friends, and family members? In particular, consider if there is any chance you are unintentionally transferring stress to those who are more easygoing in your social circles. Make sure you can unwind, or at least turn the volume down for a while, when you are around people who are likely to inherit your stress.

Play defense against inherited stress throughout the day. You have enough emotional stressors to deal with on your own, let alone if you assume the stressors of your colleagues, neighbors, and social networks.

21

Respond With Resiliency

How you react to potential stressors determines whether you will suffer the consequences. When you respond to a stressor, your body treats it as a threat. However, if you respond to the same event as a challenge, you can get a different physiological response. Responding to a situation as a stressor will leave you depleted, but reacting to the same event as a challenge could increase your energy and provide a positive charge.

As part of a large-scale study on this topic, Penn State researchers asked participants about what they had done over the past twenty-four hours for eight consecutive days. The responses allowed the researchers to see the "ebb and flow of [the subjects'] daily experiences." They also collected saliva samples to gauge levels of the stress hormone cortisol. Then researchers tracked the patients' health for over a decade.

This study revealed that participants who became upset by daily stressors and dwelled on them were more likely to suffer from chronic health problems — from pain to cardiovascular issues — 10 years later. One of the study's authors said, "Our research shows that how you react to what happens in your life today predicts your chronic health conditions [for] 10 years in the future, independent of your current health and your future stress."

It may even be possible to reframe major stressors to alleviate the damaging effects they have. A team of researchers taught a group of employees a simple three-step process for managing major stressors: First, be aware of the stress. Then, look for the meaning behind the stress (e.g., I'm stressed about this project because I know I'll get a promotion if I succeed). Finally, they asked the employees how they could channel the stress to add motivation and improve productivity.

Not only did stress levels decrease, but the participants also saw improvements in both their work effectiveness and their physical health. As one of the researchers, Shawn Achor, put it, "When we divorce the meaning from the activity, our brains will rebel." However, when you remind yourself why you are doing something challenging, your brain sees a motivator instead of a stressor.

After studying human behavior for two decades, this is what amazes me most: *Human beings are remarkably resilient* — almost irrationally so. When faced with life's most traumatic experiences, from divorce to the death of a loved one, most people have the same response. They bounce back.

It takes time, but on average, people *fully* recover from most major life stressors. Keep this in mind the next time you are dealing with something that seems insurmountable. You will bounce back. The only question is how long it will take, and that depends on your response.

Push "Pause" Before Responding

When you face an immediate and acute stressor, your instinct is to fight back and respond immediately. While this served your ancestors well when they were being attacked by a wild animal, it is less helpful today unless you are actually being attacked physically. Technology makes it much easier to exacerbate a stressor with a quick response. I know I have been guilty of responding too quickly to people, on email in particular, in a terse tone that only made things worse.

When you face a brief psychological stressor, it helps to simply hit the pause button in your mind. The more something gets under your skin, causes your heart to race, and makes you breathe a bit more quickly, the more important it is to step back before speaking or typing a single word.

If an acute stressor hits when you are reading something on a screen, it should be easier to step back and divert your attention for a while. When a person physically close to you is causing the stressful moment — for instance, when someone cuts in front of you in line — do everything possible to avoid a rash response. Not only is it likely to make things worse, but it also tells people around you that you cannot control yourself. Even under the most difficult circumstances, take a moment to gather your thoughts, and then have a rational discussion. This will give you time to think things through and determine a way to deal with the other person in a healthier manner.

Grin *to* Bear It

Making yourself smile, even if it is fake and forced, may help you get through simple stressors. I was skeptical about this concept, but when a team of researchers tricked people's facial muscles to smile, it produced real returns. The researchers trained study participants to hold chopsticks in their mouth in a way that engaged facial muscles to force either a smile or a neutral expression. Participants were essentially using the muscles required to smile without thinking about it.

When the participants were asked to work on multitasking activities that were designed to be stressful, the group that was smiling through the tasks responded better to the stressors. These group members had lower heart rate levels and lower self-reported stress levels than the participants who had neutral facial expressions. This research suggests that something as basic as smiling may reduce the intensity of the body's stress response, regardless of whether you actually feel happy during the experience.

Sarah Pressman, one of the researchers who led this experiment, said, "The next time you're stuck in traffic or experiencing some other type of stress, you might try to hold your face in a smile for moment. Not only will it help you grin and bear it psychologically, but it might actually help your heart health as well."

Another team of medical researchers has been studying the implications of the research on smiling for patients with depression. As part of an experiment published in 2014, they assigned 74 patients with depression to receive either a single injection of Botox in the "frown muscles" between the eyebrows or to receive saline solution as a placebo. Six weeks later, among the group members who essentially had their frown muscles disabled by Botox, 52 percent showed relief from depression, compared with just 15 percent in the placebo group.

Keep this in mind the next time you interact with someone who is clearly under duress. Instead of escalating your own animosity in response, force a smile and try to move on. You may trick your mind and body into a better state while avoiding a situation that will only get worse if you engage.

Epilogue:
Create a Positive Charge

The best use of an hour is to invest it in something that will continue to grow. When you add a positive charge to another person's day, it carries forward into each of their subsequent interactions. Even when you do not see the results directly, investing an hour in the growth of another person can increase the well-being of an entire network of people in the span of a day. It will also help you grow.

You are much better at helping yourself if you are also helping another person with a similar problem. Research from one of the largest clinical trials in alcohol research found that 40 percent of alcoholics *who helped other alcoholics* during their recovery were successful and avoided drinking in the year following treatment. In contrast, only 22 percent of those who did not help others were able to stay sober. Helping someone else with a similar problem nearly doubled success rates. A subsequent study found that 94 percent of alcoholics who helped other alcoholics experienced lower levels of depression.

A series of studies conducted with hundreds of college students suggests that people may be even better at solving a creative problem for another person than they are at solving the same problem for themselves. It seems that people are wired to do good and create meaning, even for complete strangers.

Share Your Most Precious Resources

Spending time on others yields a greater return than spending time on yourself. The same principle applies to how you use your financial resources. The act of giving does more for you than buying something for yourself. The good news is, you don't need a lot of money to produce happiness by giving. All it takes is a little effort.

This is the central finding from a body of emerging research: Giving improves well-being in many ways. When economist Arthur Brooks analyzed data that Harvard University collected from 30,000 families in 41 communities across America, his findings suggested that giving money to charity could (paradoxically) increase a person's subsequent wealth. As Brooks described in an address at BYU:

"Say you have two identical families — same religion, same race, same number of kids, same town, same level of education — everything's the same, except that one family gives $100 more to charity than the second family. Then the giving family

will earn on average $375 more in income than the non-giving family — and that's statistically attributable to the gift."

Every dollar given away was associated with an additional $3.75 in future income. Brooks also found that this effect held true for more than just money. People who volunteered time and donated blood were also likely to make more income in the future.

What's most intriguing about the research on giving is that it appears to be a universal phenomenon that transcends wealth in countries rich and poor. When a team of leading researchers examined data from more than 200,000 people in 136 countries, they found that donating to charity improved well-being in all parts of the world. This held true even when people reported having trouble securing food for their family.

When these researchers compared vastly different parts of the world, such as Canada and South Africa, they found that people consistently felt happier when they donated to charity versus buying themselves a treat, even when they would never meet the beneficiary of their gift. This led researchers to conclude that people are not merely donating for direct satisfaction or social connection. Instead, it appears that something deeply embedded in people's natures makes them feel better when they act altruistically.

Do Good for a Life Well-Lived

You have a limited number of days to make a difference. This is one of the few certainties that everyone shares. It can also be an extraordinary motivational force. Embrace the fact that you need to infuse a lot of good into this world while you can. You have the opportunity to decide how you will spend your time. Use this knowledge to stay focused on doing what's most important *every day.*

If you don't prioritize what's most important today, you may later find yourself wishing you had spent more time with your spouse or children. You may regret that you didn't pursue an idea you had many years ago. Fortunately, you *do* have time to add a positive charge to the world today.

Start with work that creates meaning. Invest in each interaction to strengthen your relationships. Make sure you have the energy you need to be your best. Doing these three things, in combination, is the definition of being fully charged *and* adding a positive charge to those around you.

Ideas for Action:

1. **See the Film *Fully Charged* and Share it with Friends**
   Practical ways to energize your work and life, and to improve others' well-being. Watch free clips and powerful insights from the world's leading experts.

2. **Plan for More Energy**
   Create a free 30-day Eat Move Sleep Plan to improve your energy levels.

3. **Track Your Health and Well-Being**
   Get the free Welbe app to track your daily health and energy. Compare your results with friends across platforms and wearable devices.

4. **Teach Kids**
   Read a preview of *The Rechargeables: Eat Move Sleep*, an illustrated story and program designed to help kids improve their energy and well-being.

5. **Impact Others**
   Download the Chapter Recap and Discussion Questions (next section of this book) to share and foster conversations with friends, family, and co-workers.

www.tomrath.org

TOOLS
AND
RESOURCES

A. Chapter Recap and Discussion Questions

B. Essential Reading

C. References

Note: Additional resources and PDF discussion guides for groups, teams, and organizations are available at tomrath.org

A. CHAPTER RECAP AND DISCUSSION QUESTIONS:

MEANING

1: Create Meaning With Small Wins

What percentage of your free time do you spend on activities that create meaning? How could you add one meaningful activity to your daily or weekly routine?

How did you make meaningful progress through your work today? If you did not today, how could you tomorrow?

RECAP: *Creating meaning for others matters more than pursuing happiness for yourself.*

What is the most meaningful thing you have done in the last month?

2: Pursue Life, Liberty, and Meaningfulness

Why does your current job or role exist? Does it help another person, make a process more efficient, or produce something people need?

Which external motivators tend to pull you in the wrong direction?

> RECAP: *Meaningful work is driven by deep, internal motivation.*

How could you do even more for the people you serve?

What are your best intrinsic motivators and reminders of why you do what you do?

3: Make Work a Purpose – Not Just a Place

What actions could you take that would allow you to spend more time on meaningful efforts?

Does the work you do improve your life?

RECAP: *Your work should improve your overall well-being.*

What makes you feel like you are part of a shared mission?

4: Find a Higher Calling Than Cash

Are your relationships stronger because of the job you do every day?

Is your physical health better because of the organization you are a part of?

RECAP: *Keep money from killing meaning for the sake of your well-being.*

Are you contributing to society through what you do every day?

When does money motivate you in a good way? Are there times when it steers you in the wrong direction?

5: Ask What the World Needs

What are some of the most important unmet needs among your friends, colleagues, customers, and community?

Think about your unique talents and abilities. What can you do far better than most people you know?

RECAP: *You create meaning when your strengths and interests meet another person's needs.*

What activities give you a positive charge and make a long-term contribution to society?

6: Don't Fall Into the Default

What specific tasks do you get so engaged in that you lose track of time?

Who energizes your days? How can you spend more time with these people?

RECAP: *Cast your own shadow by building your dreams into your job.*

What is one step you can take today to see how your work makes a difference for others?

7: Initiate to Shape the Future

What percentage of your time do you spend responding to emails, texts, and phone calls in a typical day? How does that compare to the percentage of time you spend initiating?

How can you work smarter instead of working harder?

RECAP: *Instead of responding to every ringing bell, focus on less to do more.*

If you could focus only on a few meaningful things tomorrow, what would they be? How can you spend less time responding?

How can you use technology to help minimize distractions instead of allowing them to disrupt you?

8: Focus for 45, Break for 15

How can you structure your day so you can work in spurts and be more effective?

How can you help remind your friends and/or colleagues about the importance of their work?

RECAP: *Work in bursts, take frequent breaks, and keep the mission in mind.*

Is there a "field trip" you and your team can take to see the influence of your work more directly?

CHAPTER RECAP AND DISCUSSION QUESTIONS:

INTERACTIONS

9: Make Every Interaction Count

What have you done to infuse positive energy into an interaction today?

What could you plan on doing in the next few hours that will add a positive charge to someone's day?

RECAP: *Our days depend on brief interactions with the people around us.*

What friends or colleagues do the best job of adding positive energy to your environment? What could you learn from them to better carry that positive energy forward?

10: Be 80 Percent Positive

What proportion of your interactions in the last day were positive? What percentage were negative?

How can you make sure that people know you are paying attention to their work and efforts?

RECAP: *Focus most of your time and attention on what **is** working.*

What is the most meaningful praise or recognition you have received in the last year? What made this recognition stand out for you?

11: Start Small and Be Clear

What small action can you take today to boost the well-being of one of your closest friends?

What is one good question you can ask new acquaintances to learn more about what's going on in their work or life?

RECAP: *Practical goals and good questions create speed and productivity.*

How can you invest even more time and energy into one of your most productive relationships?

12: Take a Break *for* Relationships

How can you build more in-person social time into your work?

Which friends and family members improve your health and well-being when you spend time with them?

RECAP: *Social networks that we often take for granted profoundly shape our lives.*

What is one practical step you could take to pay attention to other people better when you are together? How will they know they have your full and undivided attention?

13: Put Experiences First

What is an experience or trip you can plan to create well-being for yourself and others?

How can you invest more time or financial resources in the long-term growth of another person?

RECAP: *Spending on people and experiences yields the greatest return.*

How can you help others look forward to an upcoming experience or trip you have planned? If you don't have anything planned right now, what can you do to help someone else benefit from the memories of a past experience?

14: Avoid Flying Solo

What are a couple of the best moments in your life? Did they involve other people?

How much do you focus on beating a competitor compared with the time you spend trying to create new value for other people or groups?

RECAP: *We do better work when we collaborate and have shared incentives.*

Do the rewards, recognition, and incentives around you center on individual or group goals? What would the ideal incentives look like if the goal was to do more for others?

15: Build a Cumulative Advantage

What is the earliest example you can remember of someone spotting a unique talent of yours and encouraging you to spend time building on that strength?

When was the last time you noticed someone performing at an exceptional level and you pointed it out to that person?

> **RECAP:** *The more you focus on another person's strengths, the faster they grow.*

Who can you recognize in the next day with great specificity, sincerity, and detail?

CHAPTER RECAP AND DISCUSSION QUESTIONS:

ENERGY

16: Put Your Own Health First

How often do you put your own health first in the midst of a demanding day?

What could you do to build small, healthy choices into your lifestyle for good?

RECAP: *When you eat, move, and sleep well, you can do more for others.*

What changes do you notice in your mood, energy levels, interactions, and productivity on days when you eat, move, and sleep well?

17: Eat Your Way to a Better Day

What are the central elements of a healthy diet for you? How could you build more of these elements into your routine?

What are the most common foods you snack on throughout the day? Could you add healthier standby snacks to your routine?

RECAP: *Eating well starts with healthier defaults and decisions and with making every bite count.*

Do you notice how some foods influence your mood and energy more than others? How can you eat more more things that give you energy?

18: Learn to Walk Before You Run

On a typical weekday, how much time do you spend sitting? Add up the time you spend sitting while eating, commuting, working, meeting with others, socializing, watching television, and working on your computer. How could you reduce this number by at least an hour per day?

What is one thing you could start doing today to add more activity to your daily routine?

RECAP: *Being active throughout the day matters most for your health and well-being. The more you move, the better your mood.*

How can you remind yourself to take a break from sitting at least one or two times every hour, even if you just get up for 30 seconds to stretch?

19: Sleep Longer to Achieve More

What is the ideal amount of sleep you need to feel well-rested? How often do you get enough sleep to be effective during the day?

How can you make sleep a clear priority and value in your family and social and work circles? What can you do to help everyone around you structure their schedules for optimal sleep and subsequent energy?

RECAP: *Every hour of sleep is an investment in your future, not an expense.*

What is one small adjustment you can make in your bedroom to get consistently better sleep?

20: Eat, Move, and Sleep to De-Stress

Instead of focusing on one element of health at a time, what can you do to ensure you are eating, moving, and sleeping better every day?

Chronic stressors are a bigger problem than temporary stressors. How can you structure your days to avoid situations that are constantly stressful?

RECAP: *Your daily actions can keep chronic stress from accumulating and doing more damage.*

Are there specific people who create a disproportionate amount of negative stress in your life? If so, what can you do to reduce the time you spend with these people so you inherit less secondhand stress?

21: Respond With Resiliency

Identify one small stressor you have today. How can you reframe this stress (why it matters or why it is meaningful to you) in a way that adds motivation while decreasing stress?

The next time you face an immediate or acute stressor, how can you remind yourself to mentally push "pause" before you respond hastily to someone else — online or in person?

RECAP: *Your reaction to a potential stressor is more important than the stressor itself.*

What is one of the most resilient responses you have had to a major challenge in your life? What could you learn from this experience to turn your next major stressor into a more meaningful challenge?

B. ESSENTIAL READING
(ON MEANING, INTERACTIONS, AND ENERGY)

The Progress Principle: *Using Small Wins to Ignite Joy, Engagement, and Creativity at Work*
by Teresa Amabile and Steven Kramer

This team's study of more than 12,000 diary entries reveals how small daily momentum in meaningful work is what differentiates top-performing individuals and teams from the rest. This book is filled with great research on the topic of our daily work lives.

Connected: *The Surprising Power of Our Social Networks and How They Shape Our Lives*
by Nicholas A. Christakis and James H. Fowler

This book summarizes an extraordinary amount of research on the power of the social networks that surround us. Written by two leading researchers, *Connected* shows how relationships shape our health, work, and well-being in ways we never would have guessed.

Flow: *The Psychology of Optimal Experience*
by Mihaly Csikszentmihalyi

Written by one of the world's top psychologists, this book coins the term "flow" to describe the state you are in when you love what you are doing so much that you lose track of time.

Happy Money: *The Science of Happier Spending*
by Elizabeth Dunn and Michael Norton

This is the most comprehensive review I have read about better ways to spend your financial resources. Co-authored by two of the world's leading researchers and experts on spending and well-being, this book led me to rethink how I prioritize my time and financial resources.

Emotions Revealed*: Recognizing Faces and Feelings to Improve Communication and Emotional Life*
by Paul Ekman

This book will change the way you think about your next interaction with another person. Author, psychologist, and researcher Paul Ekman explores how our faces and feelings affect the quality of our days.

Give and Take*: Why Helping Others Drives Our Success*
by Adam Grant

This amazing book details why giving more is good. Written by Wharton professor Adam Grant, who has conducted a remarkable amount of research on these topics, this is an exceptional guide to building better careers, organizations, and communities.

Die Empty*: Unleash Your Best Work Every Day*
by Todd Henry

This is one of the most compelling and provocative books I have read on the topic of doing what matters most every day. Simply reading this book will motivate you to do more tomorrow.

Drive: *The Surprising Truth About What Motivates Us*
by Daniel H. Pink

This is a remarkable book about why we do what we do each day. Pink summarizes decades of important research about the need to find more intrinsic motivators in our work and lives.

Mindless Eating: *Why We Eat More Than We Think*
by Brian Wansink

If you want to make better decisions about what you eat, this book is the single best place to start. Brian Wansink is the world's leading authority on the psychology of eating and why we often make choices that work against our long-term interests.

C. REFERENCES

Prologue

1   Rath, T., & Harter, J. K. (2010). *Wellbeing: The five essential elements*. New York: Gallup Press.

2   Ravert, R. D., Calix, S. I., & Sullivan, M. J. (2010). Research in brief: Using mobile phones to collect daily experience data from college undergraduates. *Journal of College Student Development, 51,* 343-352. doi:10.1353/csd.0.0134

3   Kahneman, D., & Deaton, A. (2010). High income improves evaluation of life but not emotional well-being. *Proceedings of the National Academy of Sciences, 107,* 16489–16493. doi:10.1073/pnas.1011492107

4   Clifton, J. (n.d.). People worldwide are reporting a lot of positive emotions. Retrieved from http://www.gallup.com/poll/169322/people-worldwide-reporting-lot-positive-emotions.aspx

5   List of countries by GDP (nominal) per capita. (n.d.). Retrieved December 21, 2014 from Wikipedia: http://en.wikipedia.org/w/index.php?title=List_of_countries_by_GDP_(nominal)_per_capita&oldid=637426080

6   Surveys of 10,564 respondents created by Missionday and conducted using Google Consumer Surveys, August-December 2014. For more information on Google's methodology, visit: https://www.google.com/insights/consumer-surveys/static/consumer_surveys_whitepaper_v2.pdf

7   Executive summary – The future of millennials' careers. (2011, January 28). *Harris Interactive*. Retrieved from http://www.careeradvisoryboard.org/public/uploads/2011/10/Executive-Summary-The-Future-of-Millennial-Careers.pdf

Chapter 1

8   Surveys of 10,546 respondents created by Missionday and conducted using Google Consumer Surveys, August-December 2014. For more information on Google's methodology, visit: https://www.google.com/insights/consumer-surveys/static/consumer_surveys_whitepaper_v2.pdf

9   Amabile, T. & Kramer, S. (2011). *The progress principle: Using small wins to ignite joy, engagement, and creativity at work*. Boston: Harvard Business Review Press.

10   U.S. Declaration of Independence, Paragraph 4 (1776).

11   Mauss, I. B., Tamir, M., Anderson, C. L., & Savino, N. S. (2011). Can seeking happiness make people unhappy? Paradoxical effects of valuing happiness. *Emotion, 11,* 807-815. doi:10.1037/a0022010

12   Kashdan, T. B., Breen, W. E., & Julian, T. (2010). Everyday strivings in combat veterans with posttraumatic stress disorder: Problems arise when avoidance and emotion regulation dominate. *Behavior Therapy, 41,* 350-363.

13   Grant, A. (2013, May 13). Does trying to be happy make us unhappy? Retrieved from https://www.linkedin.com/today/post/article/20130513113934-69244073-does-trying-to-be-happy-make-us-unhappy

14   Mauss, I. B., Savino, N. S., Anderson, C. L., Weisbuch, M., Tamir, M., & Laudenslager, M. L. (2012). The pursuit of happiness can be lonely. *Emotion,* 12, 908-912. doi:10.1037/a0025299

15   Amortegui, J. (2014, June 26). Why finding meaning at work is more important than feeling happy. Retrieved from http://www.fastcompany.com/3032126/how-to-find-meaning-during-your-pursuit-of-happiness-at-work

16   Baumeister, R. F., Vohs, K. D., Aaker, J. L., & Garbinsky, E. N. (2013). Some key differences between a happy life and a meaningful life. *Journal of Positive Psychology, 8,* 505-516. doi:10.1080/17439760.2013.830764

17   Smith, E. E. (2013, January 9). There's more to life than being happy. *The Atlantic.* Retrieved from http://www.theatlantic.com/national/archive/2013/01/theres-more-to-life-than-being-happy/266805/?single_page=true

18 Fredrickson, B. L., Grewen, K. M., Coffey, K. A., Algoe, S. B., Firestine, A. M., ... Cole, S. W. (2013). A functional genomic perspective on human well-being. *Proceedings of the National Academy of Sciences, 110*, 1-6. doi:10.1073/pnas.1305419110

19 Smith, E. E. (2013, August 1). Meaning is healthier than happiness. *The Atlantic*. Retrieved from http://www.theatlantic.com/health/archive/2013/08/ meaning-is-healthier-than-happiness/278250/

Chapter 2

20 Redsand, A. A. (2006). *Victor Frankl: A life worth living*. New York: Clarion.

21 Batthyany, A. (n.d.). What is Logotherapy and Existential Analysis. *Viktor Frankl Institut*. Retrieved from http://www.viktorfrankl.org/e/logotherapy.html

22 Khazan, O. (2014, April 21). Meaningful activities protect the brain from depression. *The Atlantic*. Retrieved from http://www.theatlantic.com/health/ archive/2014/04/how-meaningful-activities-protect-the-teen-brain-from-depression/360988/

23 Telzer, E. H., Fuligni, A. J., Lieberman, M. D., & Galván, A. (2013). Neural sensitivity to eudaimonic and hedonic rewards differentially predict adolescent depressive symptoms over time. *Proceedings of the National Academy of Sciences, 111*, 6600-6605. doi:10.1073/pnas.1323014111

24 Wrzesniewski, A. & Schwartz, B. (2014, July 4). The secret of effective motivation. *New York Times*. Retrieved from http://www.nytimes.com/2014/07/06/ opinion/sunday/the-secret-of-effective-motivation.html?_r=0

25 Wrzesniewski, A., Schwartz, B., Cong, X., Kane, M., Omar, A., & Kolditz, T. (2014). Multiple types of motives don't multiply the motivation of West Point cadets. *Proceedings of the National Academy of Sciences, 111*, 10990-10995. doi:10.1073/pnas.1405298111

26 Amabile, T. & Kramer, S. (2011). *The Progress Principle: Using small wins to ignite joy, engagement, and creativity at work*. Boston: Harvard Business Review Press.

27 Pink, D. H. (2011). *Drive: The surprising truth about what motivates us*. New York: Riverhead Books.

28 Lazarus, B. (2014, June 30). The train dispatcher who defines what it means to be a gentleman. *Telegraph*. Retrieved from http://www.telegraph.co.uk/men/

thinking-man/10875975/The-train-dispatcher-who-defines-what-it-means-to-be-a-gentleman.html

29   Kashdan, T. B. (2014, July 14). 16 ways to motivate anyone: Moving beyond the notion of intrinsic versus extrinsic motivation. *Psychology Today*. Retrieved from http://www.psychologytoday.com/blog/curious/201407/16-ways-moti-vate-anyone

30   University of Exeter. (2010, September 7). Designing your own workspace improves health, happiness and productivity. [Press release]. Retrieved from http://www.exeter.ac.uk/news/featurednews/title_98638_en.html

31   Feloni, R. (2014, September 26). Why Google encourages having a messy desk. Retrieved from http://finance.yahoo.com/news/why-google-encourag-es-having-messy-153211039.html

Chapter 3

32   Work. (n.d.). In Thesaurus online. Retrieved from http://www.thesaurus.com/browse/work

33   Rath, T. & Harter, J. (2010). The economics of wellbeing. *Gallup Consulting*. Retrieved from http://www.gallup.com/services/177050/economics-well-being.aspx

34   Weber, L. (n.d.). U.S. workers can't get no (job) satisfaction. *Wall Street Journal*. Retrieved from http://blogs.wsj.com/atwork/2014/06/18/u-s-workers-cant-get-no-job-satisfaction/

35   Global workforce study, Engagement at risk: Driving strong performance in a volatile global environment. *Tower Watson*. Retrieved from http://www.tow-erswatson.com/assets/pdf/2012-Towers-Watson-Global-Workforce-Study.pdf

36   Schwartz, T. & Porath, C. (2014, May 30). Why you hate work. *New York Times*. Retrieved from http://www.nytimes.com/2014/06/01/opinion/sunday/why-you-hate-work.html?_r=0

Chapter 4

37   Dewhurst, M., Guthridge, M., & Mohr, E. (2009, November). *Motivating people: Getting beyond money*. Retrieved from http://www.mckinsey.com/insights/orga-nization/motivating_people_getting_beyond_money

38   Association for Psychological Science. (2012, June 20). Respect matters more than money for happiness in life. Retrieved from http://www.psychologicalscience.org/index.php/news/releases/respect-from-friends-matters-more-than-money-for-happiness-in-life.html

39   Anderson, C., Kraus, M. W., Galinsky, A. D., & Keltner, D. (2012). The local-ladder effect: Social status and subjective well-being. *Psychological Science, 23,* 764-771. doi:10.1177/0956797611434537

40   Work. (n.d.). In Thesaurus online. Retrieved from http://www.thesaurus.com/browse/work

41   Aknin, L., Norton, M., & Dunn, E. (2009). From wealth to well-being? Money matters, but less than people think. *Journal of Positive Psychology, 4,* 523-527. doi:10.1080/17439760903271421

42   Dunn, E. W. & Norton, M. (2012, July 7). Don't indulge. Be happy. *New York Times.* Retrieved from http://www.nytimes.com/2012/07/08/opinion/sunday/dont-indulge-be-happy.html?pagewanted=all&_r=0

43   Boyce, C. J., Brown, G. D. A, & Moore, S. C. (2010). Money and happiness: Rank of income, not income, affects life satisfaction. *Psychological Science, 21,* 471-475. doi:10.1177/0956797610362671

44   University of Warwick. (2010, March 22). Study says money only makes you happy if it makes you richer than your neighbors. [Press release]. Retrieved from http://www2.warwick.ac.uk/newsandevents/pressreleases/study_says_money/

45   Kahneman, D., Krueger, A. B., Schkade, D., Schwarz, N. & Stone, A. A. (2006). Would you be happier if you were richer? A focusing illusion. *Science, 312,* 1908-1910.

46   Vohs, K. D., Mead, N. L., & Goode, M. R. (2006). The psychological consequences of money. *Science, 314*(5802), *1154-1156.* doi:10.1126/science.1132491

47   Curran, B. & Walsworth, S. (2014). Can you pay employees to innovate? Evidence from the Canadian private sector. *Human Resource Management Journal, 24,* 290–306. doi:10.1111/1748-8583.12036

Chapter 5

48   Henry, T. (2013). *Die empty: Unleash your best work every day.* New York: Penguin.

49   Lowman, R. L. (2004). Donald O. Clifton (1924-2003). *American Psychologist, 59*, 180.

50   Rath, T., & Harter, J. K. (2010). *Wellbeing: The five essential elements.* New York: Gallup Press.

51   Rath, T. (2007). *StrengthsFinder 2.0.* New York: Gallup.

52   Hunter, J. E. & Hunter, R. F. (1984). Validity and utility of alternative predictors of job performance. *Psychological Bulletin, 96*, 72-98.

53   Nye, C. D., Su, R., Rounds, J., & Fritz, D. (2012). Vocational interests and performance: A quantitative summary of over 60 years of research. *Perspectives on Psychological Science, 7*, 384-403. doi:10.1177/1745691612449021

54   Why interest is crucial to your success. (2014, April 16). *Duke Today.* Retrieved from https://today.duke.edu/2014/04/interest

55   O'Keefe, P. A. & Linnenbrink-Garcia, L. (2014). The role of interest in optimizing performance and self-regulation. *Journal of Experimental Social Psychology, 53*, 70-78. doi:10.1016/j.jesp.2014.02.004

56   Rath, T. (n.d). Health is your business. Retrieved from http://www.tomrath.org/health-is-your-business/

Chapter 6

57   Corak, M. & Piriano. P. (2010). The intergenerational transmission of employers. *IZA Discussion Paper No. 4819.* Retrieved from http://ftp.iza.org/dp4819.pdf

58   Domenico, D. M. & Jones, K. H. (2006). Career aspirations of women in the 20th century. *Journal of Career and Technical Education, 22*, 1-7.

59   Job Crafting Exercises. (n.d.). Retrieved from http://positiveorgs.bus.umich.edu/cpo-tools/job-crafting-exercise

60   Berg, J. M., Dutton, J. E., & Wrzesniewski, A. (2008). Theory to practice briefing: What is job crafting and why does it matter? *Center for Positive Organizational Scholarship, Ross School of Business.* Retrieved from http://positiveorgs.bus.umich.edu/wp-content/uploads/What-is-Job-Crafting-and-Why-Does-it-Matter1.pdf

Chapter 7

61   Rath, T. & Conchie, B. (2009). *Strengths based leadership: Great leaders, teams, and why people follow.* New York: Gallup Press.

C. REFERENCES

62   Alvarez, M. (2009, March 31). The average American adult spends 8 1/2 hours a day staring into screens. *L'Atelier*. Retrieved from http://www.atelier.net/en/ trends/articles/average-american-adult-spends-8-12-hours-day-staring-screens

63   Sheridan, B. (2012, June 19). Is cue the cure for information overload? *Bloomberg Business Week Magazine*. Retrieved from http://www.businessweek. com/articles/2012-06-19/is-cue-the-cure-for-information-overload

64   Iyer, P. (2011, December 29). The joy of quiet. *New York Times*. Retrieved from http://www.nytimes.com/2012/01/01/opinion/sunday/the-joy-of-quiet.html

65   Woollaston, V. (2013, October 8). How often do you check your phone? The average person does it 110 times a DAY (and up to every 6 seconds in the evening). *Daily Mail*. Retrieved from http://www.dailymail.co.uk/sciencetech/ article-2449632/How-check-phone-The-average-person-does-110-times-DAY-6-seconds-evening.html

66   May we have your attention, please? (2008, June 11). *Bloomberg Business Week Magazine*. Retrieved from http://www.businessweek.com/stories/2008-06-11/ may-we-have-your-attention-please

67   Schwartz, T. & Porath, C. (2014, May 30). Why you hate work. *New York Times*. Retrieved from http://www.nytimes.com/2014/06/01/opinion/sunday/ why-you-hate-work.html?_r=0

68   Killingsworth, M. A. & Gilbert, D. T. (2010). A wandering mind is an unhappy mind. *Science, 330*, 932. doi:10.1126/science.1192439

69   Forrester, D. P. (2014, August 6). How to train yourself to stop multitasking. *Bloomberg Buinessweek*. Retrieved from http://www.businessweek.com/articles/2014-08-06/how-to-train-yourself-to-stop-multitasking

70   Say "no" to interruptions, "yes" to better work. (2014, July 14). *Human Factors and Ergonomics Society*. Retrieved from https://www.hfes.org/Web/Detail-News.aspx?ID=343

71   Classical conditioning. (n.d.). Retrieved December 22, 2014 from Wikipedia: http://en.wikipedia.org/wiki/Classical_conditioning

72   Ott, A. (2010, November 11). How social media has changed to workplace. Retrieved from http://www.fastcompany.com/1701850/how-social-media-has-changed-workplace-study

73   Kushlev, K. & Dunn, E. Q. (2015). Checking email less frequently reduces stress. *Computers in Human Behavior, 43,* 220-228. doi:10.1016/j.chb.2014.11.005

74   Barber, L. K. & Santuzzi, A. M. (2014). Please respond ASAP: Workplace telepressure and employee recovery. *Journal of Occupational Health Psychology,* Advance online publication. http://dx.doi.org/10.1037/a0038278

75   Collaborative and social tools increase employee interruptions. (2011). [Graphic illustration]. *T & D, 65*(7), 23.

76   Baer, D. (2013, August 2). What to do when email is sucking away your soul. Retrieved from http://www.fastcompany.com/3015162/leadership-now/what-to-do-when-email-is-sucking-away-your-soul

Chapter 8

77   Walker, T. (2014, June 30). How Finland keeps kids focused through free play. *The Atlantic.* Retrieved from http://www.theatlantic.com/education/archive/2014/06/how-finland-keeps-kids-focused/373544

78   Pellegrini, A. D. & Davis, P. D. (1993). Relations between children's playground and classroom behavior. *British Journal of Educational Psychology, 63,* 88-95. doi:10.1111/j.2044-8279.1993.tb01043.x

79   Gifford, J. (2014, July 31). The rule of 52 and 17: It's random, but it ups your productivity. Retrieved from https://www.themuse.com/advice/the-rule-of-52-and-17-its-random-but-it-ups-your-productivity

80   Purpose in life may protect against harmful changes in the brain associated with Alzheimer's disease. (2012, May 4). Retrieved from http://www.newswise.com/articles/purpose-in-life-may-protect-against-harmful-changes-in-the-brain-associated-with-alzheimer-s-disease

81   Boyle, P. A., Buchman, A. S., Wilson, R. S., Yu, L., Schneider, J. A., & Bennett, D. A. (2012). Effect of purpose in life on the relation between Alzheimer disease pathologic changes on cognitive function in advanced age. *JAMA Psychiatry, 69,* 499-504. doi:10.1001/archgenpsychiatry.2011.1487

82   Association for Psychological Science. (2014, May 12). Having a sense of purpose may add years to your life. [Press release]. Retrieved from http://www.psychologicalscience.org/index.php/news/releases/having-a-sense-of-purpose-

in-life-may-add-years-to-your-life.html?utm_source=pressrelease&utm_medium=eureka&utm_campaign=purposelongevity

83   Hill, P. L., & Turiano, N. A. (2014). Purpose in life as a predictor of mortality across adulthood. *Psychological Science*, 25, 1482-1486. doi:10.1177/0956797614531799

84   Stillman, J. (2013, January 15). Best way to motivate your team for free. Retrieved from http://www.inc.com/jessica-stillman/the-best-way-to-motivate-your-team-for-free.html

85   Miller, A. (2013). The science of "karma." *APA Monitor, 44*(9), 28.

86   The human impact of our work: GE staff meet cancer survivors. Retrieved December 22, 2014 from http://newsroom.gehealthcare.com/human-impact-of-our-work/

87   Radiological Society of North America. (2008, December 2). *Patient photos spur radiologist empathy and eye for detail.* [Press release]. Retrieved from http://www2.rsna.org/timssnet/media/pressreleases/pr_target.cfm?ID=389

88   Powers, J. (2013, December 26). 10 inexpensive ways to boost employee morale. Retrieved from http://www.ragan.com/Main/Articles/10_inexpensive_ways_to_boost_employee_morale_43589.aspx

89   Grant, A. (2014, January 30). Give and take: The path from independence to success. *Psychology Today*. Retrieved from http://www.psychologytoday.com/blog/give-and-take/201401/the-no-1-feature-meaningless-job

90   Grant, A. (2011, June). How customers can rally your troops. *Harvard Business Review*. Retrieved from http://hbr.org/2011/06/how-customers-can-rally-your-troops/ar/1

91   Hill, P. L. & Turiano, N. A. (2014). Purpose in life as a predictor of mortality across adulthood. *Psychological Science*, 25, 1482-1486. doi:10.1177/0956797614531799

Chapter 9

92   Diener, E., Sandvik, E., & Pavot, W. (2009). Happiness is the frequency, not the intensity of positive versus negative affect. *Assessing Well-Being, 39,* 213-231. doi:10.1007/978-90-481-2354-4_10

93   Surveys of 10,546 respondents created by Missionday and conducted using Google Consumer Surveys, August-December 2014. For more information on Google's methodology, visit: https://www.google.com/insights/consumer-surveys/static/consumer_surveys_whitepaper_v2.pdf

94   Nooyi, I. (n.d.).The best advice I ever got. *Fortune.* Retrieved from http://archive.fortune.com/galleries/2008/fortune/0804/gallery.bestadvice.fortune/7.html

95   Christakis, N. A. & Fowler, J. H. (2007). The spread of obesity in a large social network over 32 years. *New England Journal of Medicine, 357,* 370-379. doi:10.1056/NEJMsa066082

96   Fowler, J. H. & Christakis, N. A. (2008). Dynamic spread of happiness in a large social network: longitudinal analysis over 20 years in the Framingham Heart Study. *British Medical Journal, 337,* 1-9. doi:10.1136/bmj.a2338

97   Kramer, A. D. I., Guillory, J. E., & Hancock, J. T. (2014). Experimental evidence of massive scale emotional contagion through social networks. *Proceedings of the National Academy of Sciences, 111,* 8788-8790. doi:10.1073/pnas.1320040111

Chapter 10

98   Gottmann, J. M. & Silver, N. (2000). *The seven principles for making marriage work: A practical guide from the country's foremost relationship expert.* New York: Random House.

99   Glaser, J. E. & Glaser, R. D. (2014, June 12). The neurochemistry of positive conversations. *Harvard Business Review.* Retrieved from http://blogs.hbr.org/2014/06/the-neurochemistry-of-positive-conversations

100   Springer. (2012, May 24). Positive words: The glue to social interactions. [Press release]. Retrieved from http://www.alphagalileo.org/ViewItem.aspx?ItemId=120530&CultureCode=en

101   Garcia, D., Garas, A., & Schweitzer, F. (2012). Positive words carry less information than negative words. *EPJ Data Science,* 1, 3. doi:10.1140/epjds3

102   University of British Columbia. (2014, May 29). Ostracism more damaging than bullying in the workplace. Retrieved from http://news.ubc.ca/2014/05/29/better-to-be-bullied-than-ignored-in-the-workplace-study

103 O'Reilly, J., Robinson, S. L., Berdahl, J. L., & Banki, S. (2014). Is negative attention better than no attention? The comparative effects of ostracism and harassment at work. *Organization Science*. doi:10.1287/orsc.2014.0900

104 Rath, T. (2007). *StrengthsFinder 2.0*. New York: Gallup.

Chapter 11

105 Rudd, M., Aaker, J., & Norton, M. I. (2014). Leave them smiling: How small acts create more happiness than large acts. Unpublished manuscript, Graduate School of Education, Stanford University.

106 The behaviour of successful negotiators. *Huthwaite*. Retrieved from https://system.netsuite.com/core/media/media.nl?id=9041&c=1035604&h=47e-32ba37e2a3295bec0&_xt=.pdf

107 Tamir, T. I. & Mitchell, J. P. (2012). Disclosing information about the self is intrinsically rewarding. *Proceedings of the National Academy of Sciences, 109*, 8038-8043. doi:10.1073/pnas.1202129109

108 Hotz, R. L. (2012, May 7). Science reveals why we brag so much. *Wall Street Journal*. Retrieved from http://online.wsj.com/articles/SB100014240527023 04451104577390392329291890

109 Anwar, Y. (2011, September 28). Easily embarrassed? Study finds people will trust you more. [Press release]. Retrieved from http://newscenter.berkeley.edu/2011/09/28/easily-embarrassed

110 Feinberg, M., Willer, R., & Keltner, D. (2012). Flustered and faithful. *Journal of Personality and Social Psychology, 102*, 81-97. doi:10.1037/a0025403

111 Ekman, P. (2007). *Emotions revealed: Recognizing faces and feelings to improve communication and emotional life* (2nd ed.). New York: Owl Books.

112 University of Texas-Austin. (2010, October 4). What mimicking one's language style may mean about the relationship. [Press release]. Retrieved from http://www.utexas.edu/news/2010/10/04/language_relationships

113 Ireland, M. E. & Pennebaker, J. W. (2010). Language style matching in writing: synchrony in essays, correspondence, and poetry. *Journal of Personality and Social Psychology, 99*, 549-571. doi:10.1037/a0020386

114 Association for Psychological Science. (2010, December 15). A positive mood allows your human brain to think more creatively. Retrieved from http://www.

psychologicalscience.org/index.php/news/releases/a-positive-mood-allows-your-brain-to-think-more-creatively.html

115 Nadler, R. T., Rabi, R., & Minda, J. P. (2010). Better mood and better performance: Learning rule described categories is enhanced by positive mood. *Psychological Science*, 21, 1770-1776. doi:10.1177/0956797610387441

116 Friedman, R. (2014, December 2). You need a work best friend. *New York Times Magazine*. Retrieved from http://nymag.com/scienceofus/2014/11/you-need-a-work-best-friend.html

117 Rath. T. (2006). *Vital friends: The people you can't afford to live without.* New York: Gallup Press.

118 Sias, P. M. & Cahill, D. J. (1998). From coworkers to friends: The development of peer friendships in the workplace. *Western Journal of Communication*, 62, 273-299. doi:10.1080/10570319809374611

Chapter 12

119 Griswold, A. (2014, February 25). This one simple management change saved Bank of America $15 million. *Business Insider*. Retrieved from http://www.businessinsider.com/bank-of-america-call-center-management-2014-2

120 Cabrera, B. (2012, December 6). Choose your friends wisely. *Cabrera Insights*. Retrieved from http://organizationalpositivity.com/?p=1893

121 Holt-Lunstad, J., Smith, T. B., & Layton, J. B. (2010). Social relationships and mortality risk: A meta-analytic review. *PLoS Med 7*(7): e1000316. doi:10.1371/journal.pmed.1000316

122 Sheldon, K. M. & Lyubomirsky, S. (2012). The challenge of staying happier: Testing the hedonic adaptation prevention model. *Personality and Social Psychology Bulletin, 38*, 670-680 doi:10.1177/0146167212436400

123 Misra, S., Cheng, L., Genevie, J., & Yuan, M. (2014). The iPhone effect: The quality of in-person social interactions in the presence of mobile devices. *Environment and Behavior*. doi:10.1177/0013916514539755

124 Thornton, B., Faires, A., Robbins, M., & Rollins, E. (2014). The mere presence of a cell phone may be distracting. *Social Psychology, 45*, 479-488. doi:10.1027/1864-9335/a000216

125 Huseman, R. C., Lahiff, J. M., & Penrose, J. M. (1988). *Business communication strategies and skills* (3rd ed.). Chicago: Dryden.

126 Landrum, N. (2002). *How to stay married and love it: Solving the puzzle of a soulmate marriage.* Murrieta, CA: River Publishing.

Chapter 13

127 Blackman, A. (n.d.). Can money buy you happiness? *Wall Street Journal.* Retrieved from http://online.wsj.com/articles/can-money-buy-happiness-heres-what-science-has-to-say-1415569538

128 Pchelin, P., & Howell, R. T. (2014). The hidden cost of value-seeking: People do not accurately forecast the economic benefits of experiential purchases. *Journal of Positive Psychology, 9,* 322-334. doi:10.1080/17439760.2014.898316

129 Martin, D. (Producer) (2015). *Fully Charged* [DVD]. United States: Missionday.

130 Kumar, A., Killingsworth, M. A. & Gilovich, T. (2014). Waiting for merlot: Anticipatory consumption of experiential and material purchases. *Psychological Science, 25,* 1924-1931. doi:10.1177/0956797614546556

131 Thompson, D. (2014, Februrary 25). America's weird, enduring love affair with cars and houses. *The Atlantic.* Retrieved from http://www.theatlantic.com/business/archive/2014/02/americas-weird-enduring-love-affair-with-cars-and-houses/284049

132 Norton, M. (2011, October). How to buy happiness. [Video file]. Retrieved from http://t.co/sDlqruee

133 Zane, J. P. (2014). How to gladden a wealthy mind. *New York Times.* Retrieved from http://www.nytimes.com/2014/10/23/your-money/how-to-gladden-a-wealthy-mind-.html?_r=0

134 Guevarra, D. A. & Howell, R. T. (2014). To have in order to do: Exploring the effects of consuming experiential products on well-being. *Journal of Consumer Psychology.* doi:10.1016/j.jcps.2014.06.006

135 Mitchell, T. R., Thompson, L., Peterson, E., & Cronk, R. (1997). Temporal adjustments in the evaluation of events: The "rosy view." *Journal of Experimental Social Psychology, 33,* 421–448. doi:10.1006/jesp.1997.1333

136 Parker-Pope, T. (2010, February 18). How vacations affect your happiness. *New York Times*. Retrieved from http://well.blogs.nytimes.com/2010/02/18/how-vacations-affect-your-happiness/?_r=0

Chapter 14

137 Jaremka, L. M., Gabriel, S., & Carvallo, M. (2011). What makes us feel the best also makes us feel the worst: The emotional impact of independent and interdependent experiences. *Self and Identity*, 10, 44-63. doi:10.1080/15298860903513881

138 Donovan, P. (2010, August 26). Our best and worst moments occur within social relationships, research shows. [Press release] Retrieved from http://www.buffalo.edu/news/releases/2010/08/11683.html

139 Friends with cognitive benefits: Mental function improves after certain kinds of socializing. (2010, October 28). *Science Daily*. Retrieved from http://www.sciencedaily.com/releases/2010/10/101028113817.htm

140 Ybarra, O., Winkielman, P., Yeh, I., Burnstein, E., & Kavanagh. L. (2011). Friends (and sometimes enemies) with cognitive benefits: What types of social interactions boost executive functioning? *Social Psychological and Personality Science*, 2, 253-261. doi:10.1177/1948550610386808

141 Zero-sum game. Retrieved December 28, 2014 from http://en.wikipedia.org/wiki/Zero-sum_game

142 Anik, L., Aknin, L. B., Norton, M. I., Dunn, E. W., & Quoidbach, J. (2013). Prosocial bonuses increase employee satisfaction and team performance. *PLoS ONE, 8*(9): e75509. doi:10.1371/journal.pone.0075509

Chapter 15

143 Judge, T. A. & Hurst, C. (2008). How the rich (and happy) get richer (and happier): Relationship of core self-evaluations to trajectories in attaining work success. *Journal of Applied Psychology, 93*, 849-863. doi:10.1037/0021-9010.93.4.849

144 Rath. T. (2004). *How full is your bucket?* New York: Gallup Press.

145 Rath, T., Reckmeyer, M., & Manning, M. J. (2009). *How full is your bucket? For kids.* New York: Gallup Press.

146 Fredrickson, B. L. (2009). *Positivity: Top-notch research reveals the 3-to-1 ratio that will change your life.* New York: Three Rivers Press.

147 Rudd, M., Aaker, J., & Norton, M. I. (2014). Getting the most out of giving: Concretely framing a prosocial goal maximizes happiness. *Journal of Experimental Social Psychology, 54,* 11-24. doi:10.1016/j.jesp.2014.04.002

Chapter 16

148 Rath, T. (2013). *Eat Move Sleep.* Arlington: Missionday.

149 Katrandjian, O. (2012, January 30). Study finds 55 percent nurses are overweight. *ABC News.* Retrieved from http://abcnews.go.com/Health/study-finds-55-percent-nurses-overweight-obese/story?id=15472375

150 Griffiths, P., Dall'Ora, C., Simon, M., Ball, J., ... Aiken, L. H. (2014). Nurses' shift length and overtime working in 12 European countries: The association with perceived quality of care and patient safety. *Medical Care, 52,* 975-981. doi:10.1097/MLR.0000000000000233

151 Surveys of 10,546 respondents created by Missionday and conducted using Google Consumer Surveys, August-December 2014. For more information on Google's methodology, visit: https://www.google.com/insights/consumer-surveys/static/consumer_surveys_whitepaper_v2.pdf

152 King, A. C., Castro, C. M., Buman, M. P., Helker, E. B., Urizar, G. G., & Ahn, D. K. (2013). Behavioral impacts of sequentially versus simultaneously delivered dietary plus physical activity interventions: The CALM trial. *Annals of Behavioral Medicine, 46*(2), 157-168. doi:10.1007/s12160-013-9501-y

Chapter 17

153 Mozaffarian, D., Hao, T., Rimm, E. B., Willett, W. C., & Hu, F. B. (2011). Changes in diet and lifestyle and long-term weight gain in women and men. *New England Journal of Medicine, 364,* 2392-2404. doi:10.1056/NEJMoa1014296

154 Brody, J. E. (2011, July 18). Still counting calories? Your weight-loss plan may be outdated. *New York Times.* Retrieved from http://www.nytimes.com/2011/07/19/health/19brody.html?pagewanted=all&_r=1&

C. REFERENCES

155 Dreifus, C. (2012, May 14). A mathematical challenge to obesity. *New York Times.* Retrieved from http://www.nytimes.com/2012/05/15/science/a-mathematical-challenge-to-obesity.html

156 Rath, T., & Harter, J. K. (2010). *Wellbeing: The five essential elements.* New York: Gallup Press.

157 Larsen, T. M., Dalskov, S. M., van Baak, M., Jebb, S. A., Papadaki, A., Pfeiffer, A. F., ... Astrup, A. (2010). Diets with high or low protein content and glycemic index for weight-loss maintenance. *New England Journal of Medicine, 363,* 2102-2113. doi:10.1056/NEJMoa1007137

158 Hoertel, H. A., Will, M. J., & Leidy, H. J. (2014). A randomized crossover, pilot study examining the effects of a normal protein vs. high protein breakfast on food cravings and reward signals in overweight/obese "breakfast skipping", late-adolescent girls. *Nutrition Journal, 13,* 80. doi:10.1186/1475-2891-13-80

159 Smith, K. J., Gall, S. L., McNaughton, S. A., Blizzard, L., Dwyer, T., & Venn, A. J. (2010). Skipping breakfast: longitudinal associations with cardiometabolic risk factors in the Childhood Determinants of Adult Health Study. *American Journal of Clinical Nutrition, 92,* 1316–1325. doi:10.3945/ajcn.2010.30101

160 Kiefer, I. (2007). Brain food. *Scientific American Mind, 18,* 58–63. doi:10.1038/scientificamericanmind1007-58

161 Glycemic index foods at breakfast can control blood sugar throughout the day. (2012, March 30). *Institute of Food Technologists.* [Press Release]. Retrieved from http://www.ift.org/newsroom/news-releases/2012/march/30/glycemic-index.aspx

162 Leidy, H. J., Ortinau, L. C., Douglas, S. M., & Hoertel, H. A. (2013). Beneficial effects of a higher-protein breakfast on the appetitive, hormonal, and neural signals controlling energy intake regulation in overweight/obese, "breakfast-skipping," late-adolescent girls. *American Journal of Clinical Nutrition, 97,* 677–688. doi:10.3945/ajcn.112.053116

163 Taubes, G. (2011, April 13). Is sugar toxic? *New York Times.* Retrieved from http://www.nytimes.com/2011/04/17/magazine/mag-17Sugar-t.html

164 USDA Office of Communications. (2013, March 02). Chapter 2: Profiling food consumption on America. In *Agricultural Fact Book 2001-2002.* Retrieved from http://www.usda.gov/factbook/chapter2.htm

C. REFERENCES

165 United Nations Office on Drugs and Crime. (2010). World Drug Report 2010 (United Nations Publications, sales No. E.10.XI.13). Retrieved from https://www.erowid.org/psychoactives/statistics/statistics_unodc_world_drug_report_2010.pdf

166 Wade, L. (2013, March 19). Sugary drinks linked to 180,000 deaths worldwide. *CNN*. Retrieved from http://www.cnn.com/2013/03/19/health/sugary-drinks-deaths/index.html

167 Centers for Disease Control and Prevention (2012, January 13). Prescription drug overdoses — a U.S. epidemic. *CDC Grand Rounds, 61*(1), 10-13. Retrieved from http://www.cdc.gov/mmwr/preview/mmwrhtml/mm6101a3.htm

168 American Association for the Advancement of Science. (2011, May 26). Cancer cells accelerate aging and inflammation in the body to drive tumor growth. Retrieved from http://www.eurekalert.org/pub_releases/2011-05/tju-cca052611.php

169 Liu, H., Huang, D., McArthur, D. L., Boros, L. G., Nissen, N., & Heaney, A. P. (2010). Fructose induces transketolase flux to promote pancreatic cancer growth. *Cancer Research, 70*, 6368–6376. doi:10.1158/0008-5472.CAN-09-4615

170 Scientists link excess sugar to cancer. (2013, Februrary 1). *Alpha Galileo*. Retrieved from http://www.alphagalileo.org/ViewItem.aspx-?ItemId=128132&CultureCode=en

171 Strawbridge, H. (2012, July 16). Artificial sweeteners: Sugar-free, but at what cost? *Harvard Health Blog* [Web log]. Retrieved from http://www.health.harvard.edu/blog/artificial-sweeteners-sugar-free-but-at-what-cost-201207165030

172 Fowler, S. P., Williams, K., Resendez, R. G., Hunt, K. J., Hazuda, H. P., & Stern, M. P. (2008). Fueling the obesity epidemic? Artificially sweetened beverage use and long-term weight gain. *Obesity, 16*(8), 1894-1900. doi:10.1038/oby.2008.284

173 Wansink, B. (2010). *Mindless eating: Why we eat more than we think.* New York: Bantam Books.

174 American Academy of Sleep Medicine. (2013, May 7). Study links diet with daytime sleepiness and alertness in healthy adults. [Press release]. Retrieved from http://www.aasmnet.org/articles.aspx?id=3869

175 Wolpert, S. (2014, April 4). Does a junk food diet make you lazy? UCLA psychology study offers answers. (2014, April 4). [News release]. Retrieved from http://newsroom.ucla.edu/releases/does-a-junk-food-diet-make-you-lazy-ucla-psychology-study-offers-answer

176 Blaisdell, A. P., Lau, Y. L., Telminova, E., Lim, H. C., Fan, B., Fast, C. D., … Pendergrass, D. C. (2014). Food quality and motivation: A refined low-fat diet induces obesity and impairs performance on a progressive ratio schedule of instrumental lever pressing in rats. *Physiology and Behavior, 128*. 220-225. doi: 10.1016/j.physbeh.2014.02.025

177 Kain, D. (2012, March 13). More trans fat consumption linked to greater aggression. [Press release]. Retrieved from http://ucsdnews.ucsd.edu/pressrelease/more_trans_fat_consumption_linked_to_greater_aggression/

178 Golomb, B. A., Evans, M. A., White, H. L., & Dimsdale. J. E. (2012). Trans fat consumption and aggression. *PLoS ONE, 7*(3), e32175. doi:10.1371/journal.pone.0032175

179 Sánchez-Villegas, A., Toledo, E., de Irala, J., Ruiz-Canela, M., Pla-Vidal, J., & Martínez-González, M. A. (2012). Fast-food and commercial baked goods consumption and the risk of depression. *Public Health Nutrition, 15*, 424-432. doi:10.1017/S1368980011001856

180 University of Otago. (2013, January 23). Otago study suggests many apples a day keep the blues at bay. [Press release]. Retrieved from http://www.otago.ac.nz/news/news/otago041054.html

181 White, B. A., Horwath, C. C., & Conner, T. S. (2013). Many apples a day keep the blues away - Daily experiences of negative and positive affect and food consumption in young adults. *British Journal of Health Psychology, 18*, 782-798. doi:10.1111/bjhp.12021

Chapter 18

182 Owen, N., Bauman, A., & Brown, W. (2009). Too much sitting: A novel and important predictor of chronic disease risk? *British Journal of Sports Medicine, 43*, 81–83. doi:10.1136/bjsm.2008.055269

183 Blaszczak-Boxe, A. (2014, July 8). Two hours of sitting cancels out 20 minutes of exercise, study finds. *CBS News*. Retrieved from http://www.cbsnews.com/news/two-hours-of-sitting-cancels-out-20-minutes-of-exercise-study-finds

C. REFERENCES

184 Matthews, C. E., George, S. M., Moore, S. C., Bowles, H. R., Blair, A., Park, Y., ... & Schatzkin, A. (2012). Amount of time spent in sedentary behaviors and cause-specific mortality in US adults. *American Journal of Clinical Nutrition, 95*, 437–445. doi:10.3945/ajcn.111.019620

185 Lee, I.-M., Shiroma, E. J., Lobelo, F., Puska, P., Blair, S. N., & Katzmarzyk, P. T. (2012). Effect of physical inactivity on major non-communicable diseases worldwide: An analysis of burden of disease and life expectancy. *Lancet, 380*(9838), 219–229. doi:10.1016/S0140-6736(12)61031-9

186 Obese Americans get less than one minute of vigorous activity per day, research shows. (2014, February 12). *Newswise*. Retrieved from http://www.newswise.com/articles/obese-americans-get-less-than-one-minute-of-vigorous-activity-per-day-research-shows

187 Archer, E., Lavie, C.J., McDonald, S.M., Thomas, D.M., Hébert, J.R., Taverno Ross, S. E., ... Blair, S. N. (2013). Maternal inactivity: 45-year trends in mothers' use of time. *Mayo Clinic Proceedings, 88,* 1368-1377. doi:10.1016/j.mayocp.2013.09.009

188 Hellmich, N. (2012, August 13). Take a stand against sitting disease. *USA Today*. Retrieved from http://www.usatoday.com/news/health/story/2012-07-19/sitting-disease-questions-answers/57016756/1

189 Pesola, A. J., Laukkanen, A., Tikkanen, O., Sipilä, S., Kainulainen, H., & Finni, T. (2014). Muscle inactivity is adversely associated with biomarkers in physically active adults. *Medicine and Science in Sports and Exercise*. doi:10.1249/MSS.0000000000000527

190 Sitting is killing you. (2011, May 9). *Medical Billing and Coding Certification*. Retrieved from http://www.medicalbillingandcoding.org/sitting-kills

191 Clarke, A. (2014, January 13). If you're sitting down, you're a sitting duck. *Herald Sun*. Retrieved from http://www.heraldsun.com.au/news/opinion/if-youre-sitting-down-youre-a-sitting-duck/story-fni0ffsx-1226800055731?nk=e49bb-7cecc0166e4593c7afebde8ead8

192 Stairway to health. (n.d.). Retrieved from http://hsc.unm.edu/wellness/physical/stairs.html

193 Ariga, A., & Lleras, A. (2011). Brief and rare mental "breaks" keep you focused: Deactivation and reactivation of task goals preempt vigilance decrements. *Cognition, 118*, 439–443. doi:10.1016/j.cognition.2010.12.007

194 Stillman, J. (2012, July 18). *Your desk is making you stupid.* Retrieved from http://www.inc.com/jessica-stillman/be-smarter-get-up-and-walk-around. html

195 Chang, B. (2014, June 13). Can exercise close the achievement gap? Retrieved from http://www.psmag.com/navigation/health-and-behavior/can-exercise-close-achievement-gap-83433

196 Tine, M. (2014). Acute aerobic exercise: an intervention for the selective visual attention and reading comprehension of low-income adolescents. *Frontiers in Psychology*, 5, 575. doi:10.3389/fpsyg.2014.00575

197 Widrich, L. (2014, February 4). What happens to our brains when we exercise and how it makes us happier. Retrieved from http://www.fastcompany. com/3025957/work-smart/what-happens-to-our-brains-when-we-exercise-and-how-it-makes-us-happier?

198 Bravata, D. M., Smith-Spangler, C., Sundaram, V., Gienger, A. L., Lin, N., Lewis, R., ... & Sirard, J. R. (2007). Using pedometers to increase physical activity and improve health: A systematic review. *Journal of the American Medical Association, 298*, 2296–2304. doi:10.1001/jama.298.19.2296

199 Dwyer, T., Ponsonby, A. L., Ukoumunne, O. C., Pezic, A., Venn, A., Dunstan, D., ... Shaw, J. (2011). Association of change in daily step count over five years with insulin sensitivity and adiposity: population based cohort study. *British Medical Journal, 342*, c7249–c7249. doi:10.1136/bmj.c7249

200 Sibold, J. S., & Berg, K. M. (2010). Mood enhancement persists for up to 12 hours following aerobic exercise: A pilot study. *Perceptual and Motor Skills, 111*(2), 333–342. doi:10.2466/02.06.13.15.PMS.111.5.333-342

201 Knab, A. M., Shanley, R. A., Corbin, K., Jin, F., Sha, W., & Nieman, D. C. (2011). A 45-minute vigorous exercise bout increases metabolic rate for 19 hours. *Medicine & Science in Sports & Exercise, 43*(9), 1643-1648. doi:10.1249/ MSS.0b013e3182118891

202 Reynolds, G. (2014, April 30). Want to be more creative? Take a walk. [Web log]. Retrieved from http://well.blogs.nytimes.com/2014/04/30/ want-to-be-more-creative-take-a-walk/?_php=true&_type=blogs&_ php=true&_type=blogs&smid=tw-nytimeshealth&seid=auto&_r=1&&utm_ content=buffera57a0&utm_medium=social&utm_source=twitter. com&utm_campaign=buffer

203 Lenneville, E. (2013, June 6). Why do I think better after I exercise? *Scientific American*. Retrieved from http://www.scientificamerican.com/article/why-do-you-think-better-after-a-walk-exercise

Chapter 19

204 Fryer, B. (2006, October) Sleep deficit: The performance killer. *Harvard Business Review*. Retrieved from http://hbr.org/2006/10/sleep-deficit-the-performance-killer/ar/1#

205 Ericsson, K. A., Krampe, R. T., & Tesch-Römer, C. (1993). The role of deliberate practice in the acquisition of expert performance. *Psychological Review, 100*(3), 363–406. doi:10.1037/0033-295X.100.3.363

206 National Sleep Foundation. (2013). National Sleep Foundation poll finds exercise key to good sleep. Retrieved December 22, 2014, from http://www.sleepfoundation.org/alert/national-sleep-foundation-poll-finds-exercise-key-good-sleep

207 Schwartz, T. (2013, February 9). Relax! You'll be more productive. *New York Times*. Retrieved from http://www.nytimes.com/2013/02/10/opinion/sunday/relax-youll-be-more-productive.html

208 Kessler, R. C., Berglund, P. A., Coulouvrat, C., Hajak, G., Roth, T., Shahly, V., ... & Walsh, J. K. (2011). Insomnia and the performance of US workers: Results from the America Insomnia Survey. *Sleep, 34*, 1161–1171. doi:10.5665/SLEEP.1230

209 High cost of insomnia may be a wake-up call. (2011, September 1). *USA Today*. Retrieved from http://usatoday30.usatoday.com/news/health/story/health/story/2011-09-01/high-cost-of-insomnia-may-be-a-wake-up-call/50220690/1

210 Agus, D. B. (2011). *The end of illness*. New York: Free Press.

211 Luckhaupt, S. E. (2012). Short sleep duration among workers: United States, 2010. *Morbidity & Mortality Weekly Report, 61*(16), 281-285.

212 Sleepy drivers as dangerous as drunk ones. (2012, May 31). *Foxnews.com*. Retrieved from http://www.foxnews.com/health/2012/05/31/study-sleepy-drivers-equally-as-dangerous-as-drunken-drivers

213 Cohen, S., Doyle, W. J., Alper, C. M., Janicki-Deverts, D., & Turner, R. B. (2009). Sleep habits and susceptibility to the common cold. *Archives of Internal Medicine, 169*(1), 62–67. doi:10.1001/archinternmed.2008.505

214 O'Connor, A. (2012, September 10). Really? Using a computer before bed can disrupt sleep. *New York Times: Well.* [Web log]. Retrieved September 28, 2012, from http://well.blogs.nytimes.com/2012/09/10/really-using-a-computer-be-fore-bed-can-disrupt-sleep

215 University of Florida, Warrington College of Business Administration. (n.d.). Late-night smartphone use has detrimental effects on next-day work productivity. [Press release]. Retrieved from https://news.warrington.ufl.edu/faculty/late-night-smartphone-use-has-detrimental-effects-on-next-day-work-productivity

216 Lanaj, K., Johnson, R. E., & Barnes, C.M. (2014). Beginning the workday yet already depleted? Consequences of late-night smartphone use and sleep. *Organizational Behavior and Human Decision Processes, 124*, 11-23. doi:10.1016/j.obhdp.2014.01.001

217 Wood, B., Rea, M. S., Plitnick, B., & Figueiro, M. G. (2012). Light level and duration of exposure determine the impact of self-luminous tablets on melatonin suppression. *Applied Ergonomics, 44*, 237-240. doi:10.1016/j.apergo.2012.07.008

218 Paul, M. (2014, August 8). *Natural light in the office boosts health: Daylight in your office improves sleep, physical activity and quality of life.* [Press release]. Retrieved from: http://www.northwestern.edu/newscenter/stories/2014/08/natural-light-in-the-office-boosts-health.html

219 Boubekri, M., Cheung, I. N., Reid, K. J., Wang, C-H., & Zee, P.C. (2014). Impact of windows and daylight exposure on overall health and sleep quality of office workers: A case-control pilot study. *Journal of Clinical Sleep Medicine*, 10, 603-611. doi:10.5664/jcsm.3780

Chapter 20

220 Bunim, J. (2014, July 29). Healthy lifestyle may buffer against stress-related cell aging. [Press release]. Retrieved from http://www.ucsf.edu/news/2014/07/116141/healthy-lifestyle-may-buffer-against-stress-related-cell-aging-study-says

221 Puterman, E., Lin, J., Blackburn, E. H., & Epel, E. S. (2014). Determinants of telomere attrition over 1 year in healthy older women: stress and health behaviors matter. *Molecular Psychiatry*, 1-7. doi:10.1038/mp.2014.70

222 Bunim, J. (2014, July 29). *Healthy lifestyle may buffer against stress-related cell aging.* [Press release]. Retrieved from http://www.ucsf.edu/news/2014/07/116141/healthy-lifestyle-may-buffer-against-stress-related-cell-aging-study-says

223 Harris, R. (2014, July 9). Like all animals, we need stress. Just not too much. [Web log]. Retrieved from http://www.npr.org/blogs/health/2014/07/09/325216030/like-all-animals-we-need-stress-just-not-too-much

224 Ohio University. (2013, March 13). *Dwelling on stressful events can increase inflammation in the body, study finds.* [Press release]. Retrieved from http://www.ohio.edu/research/communications/zoccola.cfm

Chapter 21

225 Pennsylvania State University. (2012, November, 2). *Reactions to everyday stressors predict future health.* [Press release]. Retrieved from http://news.psu.edu/story/144952/2012/11/02/reactions-everyday-stressors-predict-future-health

226 Piazza, J. R., Charles, S. T., Sliwinski, M., Mogle, J., & Almeida, D. M. (2013). Affective reactivity to daily stressors and long-term risk of reporting a chronic health condition. *Annals of Behavioral Medicine, 45,* 110-120. doi:10.1007/s12160-012-9423-0

227 Achor, S. (2013). *Before happiness: The 5 hidden keys to achieving success, spreading happiness, and sustaining positive change.* New York: Crown Business.

228 Clark, A. E., Diener, E., Georgellis, Y., & Lucas, R. E. (2008). Lags and leads in life satisfaction: A test of the baseline hypothesis. *Economic Journal, 118,* F22-F243.

229 Association for Psychological Science. (2012, July 30). Grin and bear it! Smiling facilitates stress recovery. [Press release]. Retrieved from http://www.psychologicalscience.org/index.php/news/releases/smiling-facilitates-stress-recovery.html

230 Kraft, T. L. & Pressman, S. D. (2012). Grin and bear it: The influence of manipulated facial expression on the stress response. *Psychological Science, 23,* 1372-1378. doi:10.1177/0956797612445312

231 Finzi, E. & Rosenthal, N. E. (2014). Treatment of depression with onabotulinumtoxinA: A randomized, double-blind, placebo controlled trial. *Journal of Psychiatric Research, 52,* 1-6. doi:10.1016/j.jpsychires.2013.11.006

Epilogue

232 Pagano, M. E., Post, S. G., & Johnson, S. M. (2011). Alcoholics Anonymous-related helping and the helper therapy principle. *Alcoholism Treatment Quarterly, 29*, 23-34. doi:10.1080/07347324.2011.538320

233 Jarrett, C. (n.d). How thinking for others can boost creativity. Retrieved from http://bps-research-digest.blogspot.com/2011/03/how-thinking-for-others-can-boost-your.html#.U5nxZZRdVfF

234 Polman, E. & Emich, K. J. (2011). Decisions for others are more creative than decisions for the self. *Personality and Social Psychology Bulletin, 37*, 492-501. doi:10.1177/0146167211398362

235 Brooks, A. C. (2009, Summer). Why giving matters. *Brigham Young University Magazine*. Retrieved from http://magazine.byu.edu/?act=view&a=2441

236 Aknin, L. B., Barrington-Leigh, C. P., Dunn, E. W., Helliwell, J. F., Burns, J. Biswas-Diener, R. ...Norton, M. I. . (2013). Prosocial spending and well-being: Cross-cultural evidence for a psychological universal. *Journal of Personality and Social Psychology, 104*(4), 635-652. doi:10.1037/a0031578

The People Who Made This Book Possible

As I've mentioned, the most meaningful work in life occurs in the context of great relationships. I find it hard to believe that any decent book could be written in isolation, without an extraordinary amount of help and feedback from many other people. Over the years, I've been fortunate to work on every single book with my close friend and publisher Dr. Piotr Juszkiewicz. Once again, he has helped shape the focus, form, and function of this project for the better at every turn.

The other person who dedicated an extraordinary amount of time to this book is my wife, Ashley. She has always been the advisor I trust most with very raw material . . . to see if it even makes sense, let alone has the ability to resonate with others. Over the last year, she has read countless versions of every chapter in this book, and has done even more to help us refine the children's book we will also publish this year, *The Rechargeables*. While Ashley's contributions to these books has been invaluable, I learn even more from her every day by observing what an extraordinary friend and wife, and what an amazing mother to our two young children, she is. The meaning and energy I derive from time with Ashley and our family is like nothing I ever expected or thought was possible.

I have also been fortunate enough to have an amazing editor, Kelly Henry, who has worked on every single book and taught me to be a much better writer along the way. In addition, Krissa Lagos and Leslie Wells have made a significant contribution to editing not only this book but also other projects and articles over the past year. Edward Bobel and Brent Wilcox helped us to ensure this book's layout made it easy to read throughout, and Sherwin Soy created the jacket design.

One of the most important elements of the writing process for me is getting fairly in-depth feedback from a select group of people on my early drafts. The following team provided extensive feedback that shaped what this book has become: Jamie Blaine, Mary Cheddie, Margaret Greenberg, Dr. Maria de Guzman, Judy Krings, Dr. Shane Lopez, David Martin, Tom Matson, Lisa O'Hara, Dr. Jessica Tyler, Trish Ward, and Christine Wilkinson. Our long-term partners at Perseus—Eric Kettunen, Susan Reich, and Kim Wylie—have also been great advisors on this project and have helped ensure the book is available everywhere. And the team at Shelton Interactive designed the new tomrath.org website to serve as an even better resource to readers.

About the Author

Tom Rath is an author and researcher who studies the role of human behavior in business, health, and well-being. He has been described by business leaders and the media as one of the greatest thinkers and nonfiction writers of his generation.

Tom has written five *New York Times* and *Wall Street Journal* bestsellers over the past decade, starting with the #1 *New York Times* bestseller *How Full Is Your Bucket?* His book *StrengthsFinder 2.0* was the top-selling book of 2013 worldwide on Amazon.com. Tom's latest bestsellers are *Strengths Based Leadership, Wellbeing,* and *Eat Move Sleep: How Small Choices Lead to Big Changes.* In total, his books have sold more than 6 million copies and have made more than 300 appearances on the *Wall Street Journal* bestseller list.

In addition to his work as a researcher, writer, and speaker, Tom serves as a senior scientist for and advisor to Gallup, where he previously spent thirteen years leading the organization's work on employee engagement, strengths, leadership, and well-being. He is also a scientific advisor to Welbe, a startup that uses apps and wearable technology to improve health and well-being in the workplace.

Tom previously served as vice chairman of the VHL cancer research organization. He holds degrees from the University of Michigan and the University of Pennsylvania, where he is now a regular guest lecturer. Tom, his wife, Ashley, and their two children live in Arlington, Virginia.

www.tomrath.org

@TomCRath

silicon_guild

The Silicon Guild is a group of thought leaders and best-selling authors who write about the ideas and trends shaping business and society. The mission of The Silicon Guild is to support and empower writers, readers, and leaders alike.